morissette

death of cinderella

alanis

morissette

death of cinderella

stuart coles

Plexus, London

This book is dedicated to Krystal Welch

Published by Plexus Publishing Limited
55a Clapham Common Southside
London SW4 9BX
First Printing 1998

British Library Cataloguing in Publication Data

Coles, Stuart
  Alanis Morissette: death of Cinderella
  1. Morissette, Alanis
  2. Rock Musicians - Canada - Biography
  3. Women rock musicians - Canada -
  Biography
  I.Title
  782.4'2'166'092

ISBN 0 85965 258 0

Printed in Great Britain by
Hillman Printers, Frome
Cover designed by John Mitchell
Book designed by Phil Gambrill

10 9 8 7 6 5 4 3 2 1

Acknowledgements

For invaluable and in-depth information on
Alanis' early years, Paul Cantin's book *Jagged*
was an essential source, and is gratefully
acknowledged. His work in the *Ottowa Sun* was
also important. Other vital magazines and media
sources which need to be credited and thanked
for their help in researching this book are:
Rolling Stone, *Q*, *Spin*, *Houston Chronicle*,
Guitar World, the *Scotsman*, the *Independent*,
Pittsburgh Tribune, *Chicago Sun*, *Toronto Sun*,
Addicted To Noise, *Sunday Mail*, *Irish Times*,
Dayton Daily News, Thomson Newspapers Inc.,
Star Tribune, *San Diego Union Tribune*,
Daily Variety, the *Fresno Bee*, the *Observer*,
100.3 WHTZ Radio, 102.7 WNEW Radio,
John A. Johnson, Chris Harris, Mark Brown,
Julene Snyder, Jeff Spurrier, David Wild,
Fred Shuster, and Channel 3 News in
New Zealand.

We would like to thank the following photogra-
phers and picture agencies and the *Ottawa Sun*
for supplying photographs:
All Action, Dave Hogan/All Action; Simon
Meaker/All Action; Justin Thomas/All Action;
Ottawa Sun, Denis Cyr/Ottawa Sun; Jeff
Bassett/Ottawa Sun; Retna Pictures, Colin
Bell/Retna Pictures; Jay Blakesberg/Retna
Pictures; Steve Double/Retna Pictures; Scarlet
Page/Retna Pictures; Mitch Jenkins/Retna
Pictures; Neils van Iperen/Retna Pictures;
C.Rikken/Retna Pictures; Bill Davila/Retna
Pictures; S.I.N, Roy Tee/S.I.N; Richard
Beland/S.I.N; NGI/S.I.N; Cover photograph by
Steve Double/Retna Pictures.

contents

great expectations

"Eventually, I rejected the whole concept of organised religion, still do. But now when I'm on-stage, it's very spiritual. I feel very close to God when I'm up there."

T he 100,000 people who turned up to watch the Prince's Trust Concert on 29 June 1996 in London's Hyde Park could have been forgiven for thinking they were back in the sixties. After all, the line-up included Bob Dylan, Eric Clapton and the Who, performers who had all reigned supreme during that decade and produced some of their finest music in those liberal years. The female singer who bounded onto the stage in full Haight-Astbury regalia, complete with flouncy shirt, flowing locks and tight pants did little to change this impression. Backstage, she had just left her dressing room which was thick with joss-stick smoke and incense, where she had sat surrounded by plants and oriental rugs, meditating before the show. Furthermore, the woman in question admitted to researching the acts she plays alongside to check if 'their musical compatibility, their aura and how they hold themselves' are suitable. It was all very hippy, very Summer of Love. The only difference was that her esteemed fellow performers had enjoyed their first flushes of success some ten years before she was even born. She was, of course, Alanis Morissette, and by the end of that year she would have earned the accolade of being the most successful debut female artist of all time.

She reached this incredible pinnacle with a volley of songs that were so vitriolic, thought-provoking and pained that it would be easy to assume that her artistic creativity was borne of a traumatic childhood. Not so. Alanis' childhood was a picture of normality; at least until she was ten.

Her parents, French-Canadian Alan Morissette and his first-generation Hungarian immigrant wife, Georgia Feuerstein, had met on a playground when Alan walked up to her and said, 'I'm going to marry you.' The two twelve-year-olds became very close and, although Georgia's parents would not let her date, they spent many hours together playing badminton and hockey. Alan even started to teach her the French language.

Alan's matrimonial prediction came true some nine years later and the Morissettes set up home in Ottawa, Ontario, in the north-east of Canada. They soon produced three children: the first-born Chad in 1971, then twins Wade and Alanis Nadine Morissette, who arrived on 1 June 1974. Alan had wanted to name his little girl after himself, but he disliked Alaine or Alanna and opted for the Greek version, Alanis, after he came across it in a book about that country. He was a Headteacher and his wife was also a teacher who worked sporadically as a door-to-door saleswoman selling anything from water filters to burglar alarms.

Her father's profession meant that the first decade of Alanis' life was spent flitting from one school to the next. The first big upheaval came aged three when her parents spent three years teaching the children of military personnel in Lahr, a Canadian NATO army base in the former West Germany. The itinerant lifestyle did have some perks, however – each weekend the Morissettes would travel around Europe in a camper van, visiting Austria, Holland, Yugoslavia, France, Greece and Switzerland.

All this travelling did not unsettle the young Alanis as she shared her own little world with her beloved twin Wade. They went everywhere together, and in this way found stability in their constantly changing surroundings. Each Sunday they would obediently trot off to Church, although as she grew older Alanis came to dislike this routine immensely: 'Eventually, I rejected the whole concept of organised religion, still do. But now when I'm on-stage, it's very spiritual. I feel very close to God when I'm up there.'

The first signs of Alanis' artistic bent appeared at a very early age. At just six, she had become completely obsessed with a performance by family friends and well-known folk duo Lindsay and Jacqui Morgan at a local hotel bar. As Alanis was so young, she and her two brothers had to watch through the doors, but this impediment did not detract from her enjoyment. Seeing someone she knew perform in front of people made her realise her dreams were achievable, as she later told Paul Cantin: 'A lot of people that age are just as capable of doing it as I was, but they may watch Carole King, and Carole King may not be a friend of the family. Whereas, with the Morgans doing it and being my parents' best friends at the time, I thought it was something I could do.' A year later, she enrolled in jazz and dance classes at various performing arts colleges in Ottawa, and also played an orphan in a local production of *Annie*.

When she was nine she took up the piano. She immediately proved to have a natural talent for this instrument, inspired by her parents whom she described as 'very free-spirited, curious people'. A few months after her first lesson, she began writing her own material, drawing on the music her parents played in the house, including the aforementioned Tambourine Man, Bob Dylan. She was also a big fan of Olivia Newton John and the film *Grease*, which she had first seen during a family trip to Avignon – within days she had memorised every song and dance move. Former Wham! frontman George Michael was another musician she became enamoured with.

While at home, the young Alanis would sit in her room composing poems, and inevitably these were soon accompanied by the music she was writing. Initially, she played her creations to no-one, but in early 1984 she plucked up the courage to send a tape to the Morgans which included Madonna's 'Material girl' and one of her own compositions, entitled 'Fate Stay With Me'. Lindsay Morgan told Cantin how he was immediately impressed: 'I could hear lyrics in there. The song was all over the place. It was like there was no structure. But she had all the music and was just singing away with no instruments.' When Lindsay next visited the Morissette household, he worked with Alanis on the song and told her to keep writing new material as well. Then, while her parents were out one night, he and Alanis crept into his studio and added her voice to a track he had recorded for 'Fate Stay With Me'. When Georgia listened to the finished tape of her daughter's own song, she was moved to tears.

Taking Lindsay Morgan's advice to heart, Alanis wrote poem after poem, and amassed a collection of dog-eared notebooks full of ideas. Songs which emerged during this period included titles such as 'I Gotta Go', 'Another Sleepless Night', 'Over Now', Get With It' and 'Your Dreams Come In Time'. Lindsay told Cantin that she already seemed way beyond her years: 'She is like a sponge. When she was nine, she used to listen to Madonna . . . we were introducing music to each other. This nine-year-old girl talking to this old guy.' With his eyes on a grant from FACTOR (the Foundation To Assist Canadian Talent On Record) he took Alanis to his studio on his farm to record new material for a tape he would later present to the Foundation. He also booked a photo shoot with Alanis in sequins with sprayed-hair and a Japanese parasol, and sent the tape with these pictures off to the grant board. To everyone's delight, the members replied with a gushing letter of approval and a cheque for $3,000.

As Alanis had moved up to the Roman Catholic Glebe High School in Ottawa, her abilities were really starting to blossom. With this in mind, her mother sent her to an audition for a wacky kids show on Nickelodeon called *You Can't Do That On Television*. It was a locally produced show, but proved to be such a hit that it was subsequently syndicated internationally. Its offbeat style included many of the stars frequently covered in green slime. The show even sneaked an appearance in the film *Fatal Attraction*, where one of Michael Douglas' children is seen laughing at an episode in the background. As cast members were pre-teen, new recruits were constantly needed to replace the regulars who were growing up. At her 1985 audition Alanis was initially rejected for being too tall, but she was later recalled and offered the role.

In a forewarning of the future critical backlash that Alanis would endure, the ten-year-old received many vicious letters from female fans of the show. Alanis' character often dated the two hunkiest types and the jealousy this created amongst the show's viewers was more than evident in this hate mail.

When MTV later showed a clip of the now-famous Alanis, virtually unrecognisable as she was being slimed, the singer was not embarrassed, and she later fondly recalled her time on the show to Elvis Duran of WHTZ Radio in New York: 'It's a kids show, but actually, oddly enough, the jokes . . . were sort of adult humour. So . . . the fact that any kid could understand some of that humour just made me laugh . . . it was a good experience for me.' The puerile atmosphere on the show was not a natural environment for the ultra-mature Alanis, however, and she often found herself reading or talking to adults whilst the other cast members were playing with toys or fooling around – it was no surprise when the first series with her ended and she was not invited back. With many child actors dropping out and acquiring various anti-social habits or even jail sentences, the odds seemed to be against Alanis moving onwards and upwards from this initial step.

With amazingly advanced foresight for an eleven-year-old, Alanis saved all of her wages from *You Can't Do That On Television* (nearly $1,000 per show), plus the $3,000 grant that she received from FACTOR, and pooled them to produce her first single. She formed her own record label, Lamor Records, and with the help of Lindsay Morgan and Rich Dodson, formerly a member of Canadian country band the Stampeders, pressed up

*Alanis at the Prince's Trust concert in
London, 29 June 1996.*

an ambitious 1,300 copies of 'Fate Stay With Me', the song she had written two years previously.

A few local contacts managed to get the record a brief airing on local radio, but otherwise the sales were predictably low. In many senses, this was irrelevant, however. For one so young to have the talent to write a song, and the confidence and application to produce an independent single, was quite spectacular. But this was just the first step on the ladder for Alanis: 'I started making music because I could; it was never an issue of thinking that someone else should do it for me,' she recounted.

'I started making music because I could; it was never an issue of thinking someone else should do it for me.'

'I was just always writing lyrics. At first, for obvious reasons it was more creative writing and less personal. When I was nine years old I didn't have enough life experience to draw upon, and I wasn't secure enough when I was really little to be disclosing too many personal things.' Dodson told Cantin that her drive was very apparent even at this early age: 'She wanted to be a big star. No doubt about it. She was very aggressive. Very dedicated.' Even so, with his own career commitments Dodson was forced to withdraw from Alanis' progress and leave her looking for another adviser.

With the television show and a debut single behind her by the time she was just twelve, Alanis soon became a well-known face in the small local entertainment circles. At this stage, it was largely her mother who was pushing her forward, although Alanis admits she was always eager to participate.

Her progress towards becoming a global megastar took another step in 1987, when the local authorities in Ottawa started The Tulip Festival, an annual celebration of local talent in the arts. The local arts maestro Stephan Klovan was given the task of managing the event and decided to put on a kids fashion show, backed with music, in Major's Hill Park. During his preliminary auditions, he was given a tape of Alanis and her brother Wade singing by their mother and was sufficiently impressed to slot them in for an audition. He was surprised when the twins did not show up on the day, but soon after Georgia phoned in a panic to apologise for her oversight. Although Klovan was very busy organising the event, he agreed to call in at their house to finally meet the twins. He was even more interested when he was told about the girl's appearances on *You Can't Do That On Television.*

On meeting the two youngsters, Klovan was immediately very impressed by the girl, Alanis, despite her refusal to do a cartwheel for him in her yard. Like Lindsay Morgan he found she had a wisdom beyond her years: 'She was like 12 going on 30,' he told *Rolling Stone.* 'I found her very mature, you know? The thing that got me was, I knew she was a singer and I asked her to sing a song. So she sang me this song she wrote called "Find The Right Man". Here's this 12-year-old kid singing this song called "Find The Right Man"! So after she sang, I said: "This is very mature subject-matter." And she said: "Well, I wrote it."' Klovan also told Paul Cantin: 'She looked just like a nice, fresh girl. She had a nice aura about her. Even from that day, I realised she was more comfortable around older people.'

Despite the fact that singing did not feature in the original plans for the Tulip Festival, Klovan installed Alanis as the main feature. She performed in a bright-yellow dress backed by dozens of dancers and singers, and was a smash hit. Klovan watched in admiration: 'I sensed something right off the bat. There's sort of a sixth sense you have in the entertainment business. She definitely had an undefinable quality. I guess you could say star quality. I auditioned a lot of kids for that show and I've auditioned lots of performers over the years, and very few stand out with that little whatever it is, and she definitely seemed to have it and obviously does have it. But she had it way back then.'

teen

queen

"No regrets. Growth. Give yourself credit. Everybody is different. Their view of you may not be correct. Don't be perfect, be excellent. Falter. Balance. Be grateful. Be real. Never give up. Don't be afraid. I believe in you."

Klovan decided to take the young Alanis under his wing and started booking her appearances at various local events as a means of giving her both experience and mass exposure. At the same time he began coaching her in the rudiments of singing, performing and the entertainment business in general. He felt that Alanis was dedicated and talented and had a solid and supportive family behind her; with his acumen, the package had great potential.

One of the first big bookings he made for Alanis (with Wade) was a job as the so-called 'Dalmy's Kids', the models for a local chain of clothing shops. Within weeks, Alanis and Wade were plastered on posters all over town and Dalmys even let Alanis compose the theme tune for their radio advertisements. Shortly after this engagement, Alanis confirmed that her talent was growing by winning a prestigious regional talent contest.

The biggest break of all at this time came when Alanis was booked to sing the national anthem 'O Canada' at the 1988 World Figure Skating Championships in Ottawa, which Klovan had become involved in as a former champion skater himself. Alanis duly belted out the anthem to great applause. As Klovan recalls: 'The experience of singing the national anthem in front of tens of thousands of people . . . gave her a high level of confidence and exposure that is very beneficial for her now. She wouldn't want to go back and do that now at this stage, but it certainly hasn't hurt her. I think she realises that now.'

Amongst the many people who were impressed by Alanis was one of her backing band, Leslie Howe, who was known as one half of the popular Canadian synth-pop duo One To One. Howe's partner in One To One, Lousie Reny, had initially been approached by Alanis after a Sunday mass where she was singing, and with a little encouragement from Alanis' mother Georgia, a meeting was arranged. 'So I went. I felt like an idiot' Reny told Paul Cantin, 'But I just liked Alanis, because she was so sweet.' At that brunch meeting, Reny told Alanis to forget joining bands as she was too young, and instead advised her to keep writing her own material.

Leslie Howe, producer of Alanis' first two albums.

At that time, Leslie Howe was unaware of his partner's associations with Alanis, but when Georgia overheard his name being discussed in a restaurant, she asked for a phone number and called him up. Once he heard the tape, which included several original compositions as well as a cover of Bette Midler's 'The Rose', he decided to get more involved: 'She had a great voice. She had a great personality. And I just sensed she's pretty cool for her age.' He went on, 'I wasn't thinking: "Hey, we're going to be millionaires, and we're going to sell millions of records." I don't know if anybody thinks like that. It was more like "hey, this girl is good, she can sing good, she has talent, she's got a great personality and great looks. Perhaps we can do something together."'

Howe and Klovan agreed that they should pitch Alanis at the fashionable female teeny bop market. At the time Debbie Gibson was enjoying international success with her bubblegum pop songs like 'Shake Your Love' and 'Electric Youth', and her rival pubescent phenomenon, Tiffany, had just had a Number 1 hit with 'I Think We're Alone Now'. Alanis made these teenage sensations seem positively decrepit, so Klovan and Howe proceeded to invest hours of energy and over six figures of money into the potential star. Alanis had just turned thirteen.

Over the following five years, Alanis, Klovan and Howe worked closely together on shaping and moulding her career. Firstly, she was given more dancing lessons and taught stagecraft. Then, at Howe's expansive home studio, they worked on the music that was to match.

Another facet of his strategy was to introduce Alanis to influential society people, and she frequently found herself dressed in formal wear at gatherings where politicians, entertainers and noted figures were in attendance. In one instance, she even went to the home of Canada's Prime Minister, Brian Mulroney.

The first national fruits of this hard work came with an audition for the popular television talent show *Star Search*, where Alanis performed a cover of the Osmonds' 'One Bad Apple', which was adapted for a female singer and cut to 45 seconds to fit the television programming. Despite having failed an audition for the show in the past, this time Alanis was selected for the television programme and a shot at the $50,000 first prize. With the requested twelve songs finely honed (each week's winner went on to be challenged at the next show), Alanis, Klovan and Howe felt very confident, but in the end her rendition of 'One Bad Apple' was only good enough for second place.

With this disappointment behind them, the thoughts of the Alanis camp turned towards obtaining a recording contract. Howe and Klovan decided that a demo tape would not sufficiently capture the enigma that they felt they had, so, at great expense, a trip was arranged to Paris, where a promotional video for Alanis' song 'Walk Away' was to be filmed: 'We felt we had to give Alanis an international, street-smart look,' Klovan told Paul Cantin, 'as if she was this hot rock-chick who had been around the block a few times. We didn't want to play up the part that she came from this perfect Catholic family.' Having modelled for Dalmy's catalogue and even made some personal appearances at their stores, the video wardrobe was sorted out, and free hotel rooms were arranged with The Hilton International in exchange for featuring the hotel in the footage.

The video was resourceful, if rather cheesy stuff, with Alanis dancing in front of the Eiffel Tower, but at least they had managed to produce a near-professional presentation for a fraction of the usual cost. The musical backdrop was pure pop, with banks of keyboards, sequencers and drum machines. The biography of Alanis that Klovan and Howe had written to accompany her demo gives an interesting insight into how the two mentors were shaping her career: 'Despite her Grade 9 status, Alanis is a mature young girl with strong ambitions and beaming confidence . . . one is easily fascinated at the thought of her age.' The biography also lied by saying she had lived in Hungary, and went on to play down her age, calling her 'a spunky, street-cool European woman'.

Fortunately, their emotional and financial investment (some $15,000) paid off – after a few initial rejections, an associate of Klovan's, John Alexander of MCA Records', saw the video and signed Alanis on the spot. The contracts were completed on Valentine's Day 1990. Alanis was just fifteen.

One of the first things that changed when Alanis signed to MCA was her stage name – she became Alanis Nadinia, and her early promotional material for the record company introduced her thus. Within six months, however, it was clear that people found the spelling confusing and difficult to remember, so the second half was dropped.

While all this was going on Alanis was still at the Roman Catholic Glebe High School. Far from earning her extra friends, her growing celebrity caused a great deal of envy and tension at school, a situation which was exacerbated when the Headteacher took to playing her version of the national anthem at the end of each morning's assembly: 'I thought playing [the national anthem] one time was cool,' Alanis told Paul Cantin of the *Ottawa Sun*, 'but they kept playing it and it became an opportunity for daily showings of jealousy. Any time it was played, I knew there were people being really cruel, just being very verbal about what they thought. If they didn't want to hear it, that's one thing, but the extent they went to show they didn't want to hear it was ridiculous.' When she joined a covers band called the New York Fries to gain more live experience this made her yet more notorious. It was her brother Wade who bore the brunt of the abuse, however – the bullies were frequently too spineless to jeer her to her face and so picked on her less confident brother instead.

Fingers crossed: Alanis before the 1992 Juno Awards.

The problems at school peaked when her debut album, *Alanis*, was released by MCA. By now, the back-biters were having a field day and even some of her schoolteachers disapproved of her fledgling career so much that they made life very difficult for the youngster. Once again, however, Alanis was surprisingly mature: 'I was hurt a lot by it, but at the same time I didn't feel I was doing anything wrong. It's one thing when you're upsetting people because you're doing something dark and cruel. But I knew I was doing something musical and creative and that's as pure as it was. I wasn't doing anything wrong, so if people were or are upset with me, it's for their own reasons.'

The debut album for the fourteen-year-old marked the end of her brief spell in the New York Fries, and also represented a more controlled approach to her career. As Klovan recalled to *Rolling Stone*: 'She was trying to please too many people. She was recording, I had her booked all over the place [including a one-off support slot to fleetingly successful white rapper Vanilla Ice], not only singing the national anthem, but all sorts of events. And then she was performing with the New York Fries, and she found she had to make a decision to be a little more selfish and not try to please so many people.' It was a wise choice – her debut album was a big hit.

Alanis was chock full of synthesisers, drum machines, computer-generated music and sequenced vocals, and the song titles were equally mechanical to match, 'Human Touch', 'Feel Your Love' and 'Oh Yeah!' Alanis co-wrote much of the lyrics, but Howe masterminded the work, which had taken over seven months to complete. On its release, comparisons were immediately made with Debbie Gibson and Tiffany, and despite claiming ambitions to the contrary, Klovan's words seemed to justify this rather obvious parallel: 'She never wanted to be a Tiffany or Debbie Gibson. But people kind of naturally compared her to them, just because of her age and the pop princess thing. We never tried to emulate them, but they were so successful, we kind of used them for a guideline for what she was doing. If it is working down in the States, maybe it could work in Canada. That was our initial attack. I've never seen Alanis as a teenybopper artist. Even back then, the Debbie Gibson stuff and Tiffany was wimpy, sort of bubblegum girly stuff.'

Whatever their motives, the success of the *Alanis* album far surpassed even the ambitious hopes of MCA. Within months the album had passed the 50,000 mark, and Alanis was surprised with her gold disc by executives from the record company whilst singing in front of 40,000 people at the half-time show for a Rough Riders football game. The record eventually went on to sell double platinum, or 200,000 copies.

All three singles from the record – 'Feel Your Love', 'Plastic' and 'Too Hot' – were also big successes. 'Too Hot', in particular, received massive radio airplay and made the Top Ten, alongside Paula Abdul and Janet Jackson, two acts whom Alanis' managers had conspicuously moulded her around from day one. Indeed, they actually took Alanis to a Janet Jackson concert in Toronto to show her the way things could be done. The video for the 'Feel Your Love' single had a budget of $45,000, a sign that Alanis was really starting to generate some serious business. The actual promo itself took 40 hours solid to record, and showed a scantily clad Alanis dancing around even more naked, muscle-bound hunks.

Promotional tours were arranged all over the country, including one sponsored by a shampoo manufacturer, and Alanis was so professional and affable that music business types across Canada warmed to her straight away – she shook all the right hands and accepted all the sycophantic compliments with grace and a smile. She also continued to appear at the many increasingly tacky public appearances which Klovan and MCA arranged, including serving at a McDonald's drive-thru window for a charity fundraiser. Another peculiar engagement for her at this time was to be the musical accompaniment onboard the team bus for the National Hockey League new-comers The Senators. Dozens of articles were written about her, including one in the big selling *Toronto Sun* which quoted Alanis as saying, 'I love Janet Jackson and Madonna, but I want Alanis to look like Alanis,' and went on to describe her as 'a 5' 4" dynamo' and talk of her gruelling daily fitness regime.

More success still was to come – by the year end she was nominated for three coveted Juno Awards, the Canadian equivalent of the Grammys or Brit Awards. She was up for Single of the Year, Best Dance Record and the one she eventually won, Most Promising Female Vocalist. Alanis was still only seventeen.

An interesting small diversion for Alanis came at this point when she appeared in two screen productions about life at school. In the summer of 1992, she presented *Borderline High*, a documentary encouraging kids to pursue education. She then appeared in *Boys Will Be Girls*, a film about bullying in which she briefly acted and also provided much of the soundtrack.

With such a success on their hands, MCA did what all self-respecting record companies do – they banged out another album in double-quick time. The eponymous debut LP was followed by the slightly more

considered *Now Is The Time*. Alanis took a greater role in the writing of this record and clearly explained that she wanted it to be less dance-oriented and more emotionally revealing and personally intense. There were signs of a more mature Alanis, with the lusty 'The Time Of Your Life' and the philosophical '(Change Is) Never A Waste of Time', but the end-product was in many ways a mere re-hash of the first album. The synths and computer magic were still there and the album did little to break Alanis' reputation as the Canadian Princess of Pop.

The sleeve of *Now Is The Time* had a small piece of poetry from Alanis herself which read, 'No regrets. Growth. Give yourself credit. Everybody is different. Their view of you may not be correct. Don't be perfect, be excellent. Falter. Balance. Be grateful. Be real. Never give up. Don't be afraid. I believe in you.' Unfortunately, the public did not really believe in Alanis – as is often the case with acts of this nature, the follow-up album was considerably less successful than its predecessor. Although the opening single, 'An Emotion Away' enjoyed a chart placing above U2 and Bon Jovi, sales of the album were disappointingly quiet, despite Alanis still enjoying a high public profile. The record did eventually pass the 50,000 mark, but with notably less ease than *Alanis*.

Alongside the grumblings of discontented MCA men was the gradually surfacing unease of Alanis herself. From the start of her career, when she was only thirteen, every decision and manoeuvre had been made for her. At first she was happy to go along with that, bowing down to the experienced heads around her. But now, with her growing age, she was feeling distinctly unhappy with the situation. There were several reasons for this. Firstly, the music she was now singing was not what she was hearing in her head – the themes and musical accompaniments were far too superficial and lightweight. Secondly, she was extremely uncomfortable with her frizzy permed, beautifully made-up image, and the heavy emphasis that was being put on her increasingly womanly figure. Thirdly, she was tired of the endless PAs and wanted to start actually singing live, performing some of her own songs her way in front of a more discerning audience. Finally, she was exasperated by the impact her celebrity continued to have on her private life, with school life and study proving increasingly difficult, and her youthful love life being unnecessarily complicated by either hangers-on or jealous detractors.

Ironically, the first time she realised that she was unhappy with her success was at the prestigious Juno Awards back in 1992: 'That was the beginning of me going, "This is all an illusion." I think I was pretty overwhelmed that night. Society leads you to believe that if you achieve

Alanis returns home after winning the Juno Award for the most promising female artist.

this success, whether it be winning awards or selling millions of records – or at that time, thousands of records – everything is great, and you get approval from people. And is this not what a perfectionist seeks? Someone who is young and somewhat given into what society has asked of them. Is this not the epitome of what they yearn for? And then you achieve it, and nothing is different.'

To add to this artistic dissatisfaction, the pressures of the business were taking their toll on the still very young Alanis. There were a lot of people depending on her for their own careers and livelihoods, and the expectations were enormous. When she expressed a desire to do things differently, she was quickly silenced, as a teenager who was enjoying great success and who knew nothing that could improve on that position.

Alanis began to crave a normal teenage life, a best friend her own age or maybe even a boyfriend who would understand her worries. She was surrounded by people much older than herself all of the time. Many of her best friends were approaching middle-age and she found mixing with people of her own age group difficult, finding them immature or boring. Even a brief relationship she had at the time was with an entertainment person, Dave Coulier, star of the TV shows 'Full House' and 'America's Funniest People', who was almost twice her age – she called him, rather prematurely, 'the love of my life'. She also developed a habit of stealing her older friends' boyfriends, only felling desirable if they left their partners to be with her (a past she is utterly ashamed of).

She became so frustrated that she had a breakdown at her parents' house one day, when the pressures and the difficulties of life as a teenage star finally proved too much. Months of therapy helped her to regain her confidence, as she told Paul Cantin: 'I think the whole way that I was in the past was a passive–aggressive thing, where I would just sit there quietly and listen to a whole lot of things I didn't necessarily believe in, and work in environments that were really negative and difficult.' So even during the Juno awards ceremonies and the platinum disc presentations, the smile and chirpy demeanour were already a facade. Alanis wanted out.

Whether she would be able to get out was another matter. For a start, history was not on her side. When Debbie Gibson attempted to transform herself from squeaky-clean pop starlet into a bondage-clad sex siren, her career plummeted. Music history was littered with dozens of teeny bop names who had tried to change and mature only to see their success terminated with undue and often painful haste. Her childhood hero George Michael was one of the few players who had managed to escape the clutches of pure pop, turning himself over the course of a decade from a shuttle-cock touting teen sensation into a mature, accomplished songwriter of international repute. Whether Alanis could do this seemed in some doubt.

Behind the smile the seventeen-year-old star was deeply unhappy.

To make matters worse, the music world was changing dramatically. While *Now Is The Time* had been achieving moderate sales, Nirvana's epoch-defining *Nevermind* had changed the face of mainstream music. Alternative was now acceptable: both the single and album charts were crammed with grunge acts and the so-called 'slacker' culture was everywhere. It was probably just as well that Alanis decided to make a break from her suffocating past when she did – had she released yet another album of sterile pop she could well have become a laughing stock.

welcome to L.A.

Before things got better they got worse. Realising that she actually hated much of what she had been through, Alanis set about wiping the slate clean. She terminated her partnership with Klovan and Howe and found herself a new manager, Scott Welch, a former road manager and sound engineer. Welch was actually asked by MCA to find a licence for Alanis' first two albums in the US, but fortunately his views on this matched hers. He too was unconvinced that she could sustain her current style of performance and instead told MCA that they should keep her publishing rights and let her to go away and write songs as she wished. It was a remarkable piece of foresight, and one which ultimately paid off on a scale no-one could have expected.

Welch advised a change of scene: 'I said, "Let's move her out of the house, away from Ottawa, some new surroundings, and let's get some new life experiences, because that's what people write from." So we moved her to Toronto, and she got a really crummy apartment, just like most of us did when we were 18, and she got by on macaroni and cheese.'

As soon as she was settled in her new home in the Beaches neighbourhood of Toronto (in what she called 'my bohemian little apartment'), Alanis started to look around for new songwriting partners. Over the next two years of fruitless searching she got through an incredible 100 potential cohorts, all of whom proved to be completely incompatible. Her frustration at this was worsened by the financial difficulties she experienced – despite her two reasonably successful albums, 'Alanis Ltd' had never actually recouped the vast sums the record company poured into her promotion, so she received no further money other than advances and recording costs and had to get by with occasional subs from Welch or Alexander. She later told *Spin*: 'I was finally in a position where things weren't working out. And it was good for me. It made me realise that certain people I'd blindly trusted let me down. My intuition was saying "Don't trust these people, don't work with these people," and I went against it . . . I've had people cheat me out of a lot of money. Let's just say that I'm still paying for the mistakes I've made. I think of it as my tuition for The College of Music Career.' She did not point the finger at Howe or Klovan, it should be added.

The twelve months in Toronto were also a turbulent time in Alanis' love life, with the teenager going through several difficult relationship break-ups (which would later provide her with material for her *Jagged Little Pill* album). She openly admits that this was a sexually liberal time in her life, as well as the first time she actually had intercourse, transforming her into what she now calls 'a very sexual person'. Although she had been sexually active when she was only 15, she claims that she didn't actually lose her virginity until aged 19, a duality that she puts down to her repressive Catholic upbringing. It was also a backlash against the self-imposed strictures that she had endured during her time on MCA – she consciously never allowed herself to 'go off the path' and even said that she would never have taken drugs because 'that would have meant that I wasn't perfect'.

For now, however, she found it difficult to be so objective. It was a miserable time. Even a role as a rock star called Alanis in the television movie *Just One Of The Girls*, which co-starred future *Friends* heartthrob Matt LeBlanc as her boyfriend, proved to be an embarrassing flop. Most painful, however, was the continued failure to find a new musical collaborator. Every time she explained her song ideas and lyrical themes to the (mostly male) musicians, they would denounce them as 'too personal, too specific' and explain that if she wanted to achieve mainstream success she really had to be far more universal and less intense. 'There are so many disowned songs of mine out there that I have absolutely no connection with,' she told *Rolling Stone*. 'I worked almost seven days a week, writing with everybody, trying to get into the whole songwriting part of it. I would write alone, write with people, write with three people and demo, and I just tried everything. There was really no one I was connecting with in a cerebral, creative way at all. It became very disheartening.'

The strain began to tell again, and Alanis started to suffer black-outs, crying outbursts and panic attacks. After a year of failure, she could take no more and uprooted again, this time moving to Los Angeles. Entering the country described by immigration as 'an alien with special talents', Alanis initially enjoyed even less success than she had in Toronto. Her quietly spoken Canadian reserve was mistaken for passivity and she was mugged at gunpoint after only four days in the so-called City Of Angels. Her assailants ordered her to lie on the floor and not look up whilst they rifled through her belongings. Interestingly, the only thing that she was scared about was having her precious lyric book stolen, which included some of the work that would later appear on her third album. The policewoman who attended to Alanis after the attack took a few notes, said it was highly unlikely they would find the muggers and left with the parting shot 'Welcome to L.A.'

Based in Beachwood Canyon in Hollywood, Alanis' mood darkened – she continued working with songwriters with no success whatsoever, and even played a few small open mike gigs to keep her voice in practice. Then, on a flight from Los Angeles back home one Christmas, the artistic difficulties, the personal frustrations and the impact of life alone in the world's wildest metropolis suddenly exploded. She was writing Christmas cards and suddenly broke down, crying uncontrollably and feeling desperately unhappy and ill from the anxiety attack. 'It scared the living shit out of me,' she later said.

Alanis contacted a doctor and underwent several spells of hypnosis and therapy, during which many of her pent-up feelings and repressed emotions from her bizarre teenage years spilled out. It was a turning point. She moved from Hollywood to the calmer west side of the city and continued working on her music. After a few more unsuccessful partnerships, she began to enjoy the L.A. lifestyle, and even relished the emotional rollercoaster she was on: 'It's the epitome of craziness. [L.A.] Yeah, it is. It's good for me, though. It's sort of enabled me to tap into a different side of myself that I hadn't allowed myself to do in Canada.'

Welch would receive frequent phone calls from the writers that Alanis failed to jell with, and invariably they would suggest that, despite their lack of chemistry, Alanis had something. When she brought him a tape of fifteen song ideas she had been working on he saw the first signs of her future style emerging: 'You could start to see into *Jagged Little Pill*. You could see glimpses of things. I said: "Man, you are on the right track. Just stay with it."' Central to this new style was Alanis' willingness to open up her heart and expose her emotions completely in her songs, and her experiences in Los Angeles appear to have been the catalyst for this new cathartic approach: 'Everybody has to release it somehow,' she said to *Spin*. 'If you don't, it'll take its toll on you, and it'll either be a physical thing, or all your relationships will be really negative and full of conflict or something. So you have to deal, whether you go through therapy or get into relationships, or music, or write it out in diaries. Smoking cigarettes isn't enough. There's no way around pain. That's part of the charm of being alive.'

jagged little pill

"We agreed that what was being said was more important than whether the words fit, technically speaking. There are a lot of instances where they don't fit. I don't care."

If songwriting was a numbers game then Alanis was long overdue a success. In February 1994, MCA gave her the phone number of yet another songwriter for her to approach. The initial signs did not look good. Glen Ballard was a former guitarist and keyboard player of some repute who had become a staff producer for Quincy Jones. As his production reputation gathered momentum, he began to work with some of the biggest names in electronic pop and soul. On this writer/producer's list of credits were artists such as Paula Abdul, Evelyn 'Champagne' King, the preposterously pompous David Hasselhoff and even Barbara Streisand. There was no shortage of success in his work – over 200 of his songs had been published and achieved chart success, and he had even written the multi-million selling 'Man In The Mirror' for pop's wackiest star, Michael Jackson, as well as contributing to the sales of over 100 million records. All of this made him a very credible and accomplished collaborator, but not, at first glance, the man to sympathise with Alanis' growing desire to break away from mainstream pop. What's more, he was already middle-aged and a family man, as so many of Alanis' previous colleagues had been. First impressions are important and often very telling, but in this instance they could not have been more wrong.

Glen first met Alanis Morissette at his home studio in Los Angeles. Louisiana-born Glen had not heard any of Alanis' previous work, and later admitted to only being 'not uninterested' in seeing her. So, in many ways, his scepticism was probably even greater than hers. Incredibly, however, there was an instantaneous chemistry between the two strangers.

'I walked into the studio and the spirit was so warm,' Alanis told *Rolling Stone,* 'so positive. My intuition told me this was a good person. My intuition told me the music would be great, too.' Glen was similarly bowled over: 'She came to my studio, and we started writing about fifteen minutes later. It was clear to me that she was articulate and intelligent and it was just . . . we just dove right in. I think there was an instant rapport, immediately. It wasn't awkward for any length of time. It was relaxed. It really is hard to tell you why. All I can tell you is it was one of those instant connections, and we didn't have the slightest problem getting to work. That never happens. But in this case, that is exactly what happened.' Despite the plethora of talent he had worked with in the past, he also felt a unique bond with the singer almost half his age: 'I'd connected with people before but never that quickly and never that completely. My first thought was "what a voice!" then within half an hour we were writing a song.' The age difference was never a problem either, as Alanis told the *Dayton Daily News*: 'There is a part of me that's 40, and there's a part of him that's 20. We met somewhere in the middle in a very spiritual place. He and I are both ageless.'

My intuition told me this was a good person. My intuition told me the music would be great, too.

After all the waiting and trying, Alanis could not believe that at last she had found someone who not only understood where she was coming from but actively encouraged her to pursue her goals. Where other writers had told her she was too personal and too specific, Glen said she should write exactly what she wanted. Whilst others had warned against the use of too much rock and overly aggressive lyrics, Glen loved both and if anything exaggerated these aspects of the songs. Alanis explained to the *Chicago Sun Times* her feelings about that initial contact with Glen: 'Musically and lyrically, it was just so pure and so spiritual for me. I felt that he wasn't judging me, and I felt that he had enough security within himself to give the ball to a 20-year-old and let her go with it.' She continued to *Mojo*: 'Glen and I were so on the same wavelength it all came together. It was all very visceral – and fast. What makes this relationship so magic for me is that a lot of what I would be talking about or thinking about or intellectualising about – over-intellectualising about – Glen,

1992 was a turning-point in Alanis' life and career.

'Sometimes on-stage I'm like a mirror, my music becomes less about me and more about what the audience see in me that reminds them of themselves.'

Alanis after the 1995 MTV Video Music Awards in New York.

would say, "Well, yeah?" to when most people would be, "What are you talking about?" or, "God, would you stop analysing!" We'd talk, and out of the conversation would come a song. We agreed that what was being said was more important than whether the words fit, technically speaking. There are a lot of instances where they don't fit. I don't care.'

Working on their own in the studio (Alanis felt the songs and emotions were so deep and personal that she could never have had anyone else around), the pair found the lack of expectations for each other very liberating. Alanis was a moulded teenage pop star and Glen was a mass producer of production line, glossy, polished soul-pop. In both cases, the industry seemed to know their parameters. However, Alanis was thrilled by Glen's encouragement to write whatever she wanted and besides, neither he nor America knew much of her past. Likewise, he met Alanis at a time when he was straining to break out of the very artistic pattern which he was so well known for, as he explained to 100.3 WHTZ Radio in New York: '[in the past] . . . I wasn't using all of the artistic judgment I could bring to something. Alanis certainly empowered me to be an artist with her, to say "Do your thing." We weren't trying to write for the market, so it was extremely liberating for me to have my creativity unleashed . . . I hadn't felt there was a situation for me to pour a lot of my music into.' All of their musical baggage was left outside the studio door. These two facts made for an explosive combination.

Alanis would sit cross-legged on the floor, and Glen would sit in his producer's chair, both with acoustic guitars, and the songs just spilled out. The first ten or so tracks they wrote, including one called 'The Bottom Line', did not actually make it on to *Jagged Little Pill*, but the point was that a relationship had been struck up, and the momentum they gathered over the coming days was fearsome. The first real turning point that Alanis remembers, when the third album really started to take shape, was the reflective ballad 'Perfect': 'Glen and I were working on something else, which didn't make it on to the record,' she told *Mojo*. 'In the middle of it we turned to each other and went off on this other song which wound up being 'Perfect'. The words and music were written in about twenty minutes and we recorded it, the original demo that's on the album, that same evening. It was overwhelming. I think we finished it around one in the morning and we couldn't leave the studio till about five because . . . it was pretty scary.'

She continued: 'We were ruthless, we started a whole bunch of other songs that, technically and musically, were really beautiful. But because of the way we knew we had to write, we'd discard them. We have pieces of another 25 songs that may have been technically beautiful, but didn't have that intangible thing about it. We knew that was what our goal was; we tapped into it for the first time when we wrote "Perfect" . . . then after that, it was "OK. We've set our precedent here." It was a drug at that point.'

This pattern was then repeated on most of the album – the majority of songs were completed within two hours, and some were wrapped up in fifteen minutes. 'Hand In My Pocket' is a case in point – they had hit their first writer's block and Glen was pacing up and down the studio while Alanis was sitting, depressed, on a couch. Then suddenly, she thought about her situation and the words poured out: 'The music and lyrics were all written at the same time,' she explained, 'it felt as if it was being channelled through. We just sort of gave ourselves up to it. There was nothing conscious about the way this record is written; it was very accelerated. A lot of times we'd listen to it the next day and not even remember having written it at all.' On this track it was also the first time Alanis had recorded her harmonica playing, and impressively this was done on the first take. Other times she claimed to finish a song at four in the morning and be so overwhelmed by the creative experience that she was giddy and physically unwell.

There was nothing conscious about the way this record is written; it was very accelerated. A lot of times we'd listen to it the next day and not even remember having written it at all.

This synergy that Alanis had been searching for for so long was incredible – by writing all of the lyrics at the same time that they were both working out the music they were able to capture the feeling of the song at the moment of its creation. Since the tracks were finished within hours of their conception, the emotion and ideas that inspired them were captured forever on tape. It was a stream-of-consciousness style of writing that Alanis has since vowed to always use.

Only later did they use a few choice musicians for certain key overdubs. The Red Hot Chili Peppers' Flea and Dave Navarro appeared on 'You Oughta Know' and keyboardist Benmont Tench also chipped in, but otherwise the original musical creations were pretty much left as they were. Within a matter of weeks of meeting each other, most of the tracks that were to make up *Jagged Little Pill* were complete.

'I've got one hand in my pocket/And the other one is giving the peace sign.'

maverick

"I respect Madonna very much. I respect her strength and her resilience in a crazy business. I still remember seeing her in an interview when I was younger, talking about freedom at a time when I was coming to terms with my own sexuality. She's a great CEO."

Before they could unleash the record onto the world, however, there was one very major obstacle to be navigated – Alanis did not have a record deal. Her contract with MCA was now only for publishing and the entire *Jagged Little Pill* sessions were completed in the knowledge that the songs might very well never see the light of day. Once she and Glen realised the potential of what they had created, they took the tapes to Scott Welch and he began scouting around for a contract.

Incredibly, in the light of later mega-record sales, the response from the industry was far from rabid. Glen sent a tape to a friend at Atlantic but he was largely uninterested. Of all the major labels they approached only four expressed any serious interest. In the course of the search, Alanis and Glen had to endure embarrassing corporate platitudes and opinions with a smile, something that Alanis in particular found very tiring. Whereas Glen was an old campaigner and it was no problem to him, she found it all very inflammatory – during this contract search she wrote 'Right Through You' which was a vicious lambasting of these record company executives.

Part of the problem was that she was a woman in an industry that is still inherently sexist. Her age also put many people off: they preferred to go with the safer bet of a rock dinosaur instead. Also, she was unusually open with her songs and her personality, and that made people nervous. Similarly, she did not always bite her tongue when the executives were talking nonsense, and several times she returned to her manager's office distraught and in tears at the experience. She found it particularly difficult when the executives started to tell her how she should change artistically if they were to make millions out of her: 'For me this was not about money or getting patted on the back. I met with some people who'd tell me, "Why don't you change this lyric, and the kids will respond more." And I'd say, "I didn't write it for them. I wrote it for me."'

Fortunately, Maverick, the label that Madonna had set up as part of her own contract with Warners, understood Alanis perfectly. Their A&R man was the extraordinary 22-year-old Guy Oseary, protege of the label head Freddy DeMann, who seemed to lock on straight away what she was doing. Glen played him a tape of 'You Oughta Know' and 'Perfect' and he listened quietly, trying to contain his excitement. When the songs finished he left the room and immediately told his superiors, Freddy DeMann and Abbey Konowitch. They listened but were not totally convinced, saying they would need to see her live before they could make any commitment. Alanis was more than happy to oblige: 'I'd had enough of meeting with people who have no concept of what the creative process is about and no respect for it, I had lost patience with that. It was really refreshing to go into an office where someone was so focused on the music.' Oseary himself said, 'She and I are about the same age, and people are always so amazed that we've accomplished anything since Generation X-ers are supposedly not ambitious. We're showing people we're as ambitious as anyone else.'

A concert was arranged in Glen's studio for a small group of Maverick executives, including Madonna herself. Glen strummed his acoustic guitar and Alanis sang a naked vocal right there in front of them. After only twenty minutes, the executives said they had heard enough and asked Glen and Alanis into the hallway. The deal was struck there and then.

Alanis was particularly pleased to be involved with the world's premier female performer: 'I respect Madonna very much,' she explained to David Wild. 'I respect her strength and her resilience in a crazy business. I still remember seeing her in an interview when I was younger, talking about freedom at a time when I was coming to terms with my own sexuality. She's a great CEO.' Madonna herself was very excited with her new charge: 'She reminds me of me when I started out: slightly awkward but extremely self-possessed and straightforward. There's a sense of excitement and giddiness in the air around her – like anything's possible, and the sky's the limit.'

*   *   *

With the album scheduled for a June 1994 release, the taster single 'You Oughta Know' was put out. Despite the highly creative and richly productive sessions that Glen and Alanis had enjoyed at his home studio, and despite Maverick's hopes for their new artist, no-one could possibly have imagined the impact that this one song would have. Almost single-handedly, 'You Oughta Know' took Alanis Morissette from relative obscurity to the front covers of the world's music magazines and the top of radio playlists.

The signs that this single was something special were immediately apparent. Even before it had been issued to radio stations, it was included on a magazine compilation tape and certain radio stations started playing that version. Amazingly, each time they played the track, their phones lit up with people wanting to know who the artist was and where they could buy the single. Live 105 in California claims to be one of the first radio stations to play the single, and their main DJ says the response was unbelievable: 'I have never seen a song take off like this one has.' By the time Maverick had pressed up their copies, the demand was already massive. Funnily, many radio stations who claimed to have 'discovered' the track first seemed to know almost nothing about Alanis, and one even called her Atlantis Morissette.

Looking at 'You Oughta Know', it is not hard to see why it was so successful. A four-minute vitriolic outburst against a former lover who has left Alanis for an older woman, the song was as venomous and scary as anything the American music scene had seen for some time. Starting with Alanis muttering transparently insincere good wishes to the new couple, the song then explodes into a wave of bitterness and scathingly demeaning judgements on her love rival. She talks of her replacement making a good mother, insinuates that she is sexually unadventurous and bitingly criticises the haste with which she was replaced.

The musical backdrop to this is essentially a simple, stripped down rock song, with fairly conventional rock guitars from the Red Hot Chili Peppers' Dave Navarro being mixed with a simple four note hook and meshed together with a melodic roaming bassline, courtesy of another Chili Pepper, Flea. Alanis' vocal is mixed very high, almost as if she has confronted her old lover in a public place and is talking embarrassingly loudly about her resentment.

Alanis' lyrics are filled with poisonous anger thoughout, but it was two lines in particular that caused an absolute media frenzy. In the first verse she asks the man if his new lover would go down on him in a theatre like his old 'perverted' Alanis, and then goes on to question if he thinks of her when he fucks his new woman. This last line posed a special problem for Alanis in Glen's studio sessions. Although it was exactly how she felt, she was unsure if she could be that open on record, and also if she would be able to sing the song live each night in front of a crowd full of strangers. Glen was adamant: 'He said to me, "Just remember how bad you felt when you did censor yourself. You have to do this." [That line] was 100 percent honest. For me to take that back would be telling a half-truth and I didn't want to do that ever again. It took me about a day to get over it, to let go of the fear of how it was going to be responded to.' It was a wise choice – the crude language and desire for revenge captures perfectly the emotional devastation when a spurned lover discovers that everything they had with their partner was based on deception.

What made the song even more striking was the brutal honesty of Alanis' words, and the fact that few other performers, especially women, were speaking in such honest, open terms. The mainstream rarely allowed such intense exorcisms and preferred to see such emotional pain glossed over, but here was a young woman, previously unknown in the States, whose opening volley quite simply made the industry stop in its tracks. 'You Oughta Know' was an astonishing single and a peerless debut.

In a music world where the complete package is usually a necessity, the video for the single was similarly lauded and successful. Directed by Nick Egan, the atmospheric promo was shot over three days in the wastelands of Death Valley. During the course of the song Alanis transforms from a girl crying in her prom dress to an angry leather-clad young woman, all the time filmed in soft focus, barely showing her face long enough to recognise her. She changes her clothes three times in total, symbolising the emotional skin-shedding in the song itself. The video finishes with Alanis lying down in a field of flowers, her bitterness emptied and her heart on its way to recovery. Just as the radio stations instantly loved the single, the highly influential MTV put the video on heavy rotation, and it became a constant feature of their new singles show *Buzz Bin*. Geoffrey Darby, one of her former directors on *You Can't Do That On Television*, was not so impressed: 'When I first heard "You Oughta Know", I thought, "That came out of the mouth of our sweet little girl?"'

An uncompromising stance: Alanis refused to censor
the brutal honesty of her lyrics.

Although 'You Oughta Know' was a massive hit in commercial terms, reaching the Top Five in the American singles charts and going Top Ten across Europe and Britain, in many ways, the emotional connection that Alanis had made with the public was far more significant. She suddenly found herself to be the mouthpiece for a generation of women spurned, a figurehead for a social group who were tired of keeping their pain secret. Her manager's office was flooded with fan mail saying she had given these women strength, and the precision with which she had made her own experience universal was highlighted by the fact that many letters said 'she must have known my ex'. Reflecting on having been catapulted to this position, Alanis was keen to specify her motivations for the song: 'If it was written for revenge, I think I'd be telling everyone his name,' she explained to the *Dayton Daily News*. 'I would never mention his name. That goes for any song on the record. There are a lot of people I write about, but I would never mention any names. I haven't talked to him. I have reason to believe that he doesn't know it's about him. [Now] I'm secretly grateful to him for walking away from a relationship that wasn't very healthy.' She continued in *Q* magazine: 'It had felt so excruciatingly painful it forced me to realise I had continually put my self-esteem in a man's hand. Through that I learned that I would never do that again.'

Alanis' delight at the song's success was tinged with a little sadness at the fact that so many of her fans had experienced the same kind of rejection as her: 'We didn't know this was going to happen,' she said to Elvis Duran on WHTZ: 'I had no idea. It's gratifying. On one hand, I'm sort of comforted by the fact that people can relate to it, and on the other hand, I'm sort of saddened by the fact that so many people can relate to it. It's not necessarily the most positive feeling in the world.' It was however, a very positive start to Alanis' rebirth. As a consequence of the single's huge impact, the anticipation for the forthcoming album was already beyond anything her camp could have wished for.

+ + +

Regardless of its later mammoth commercial success, *Jagged Little Pill* is a superb record in many ways. A track by track analysis reveals that Glen and Alanis' feelings of euphoria at their L.A. sessions were justified.

The opening song, 'All I Really Want' is a perfect indication of the emotional rollercoaster to come. In it Alanis opens up her views on life and love and in the process warns the listener that the record that follows will be a no-holds-barred experience, and one that by definition provides a revealing insight into Alanis herself. She talks of her need to analyse everything in the minutest detail, a trait which was probably borne out of her love of therapy and psychology, having seen a therapist herself since the age of sixteen: 'It started when I was 16 or so, and that was totally self-motivated,' she said to Paul Cantin of the *Ottawa Sun*. 'I was totally into psychology. If I wasn't a musician, I'd be a psychologist. Not only to benefit me. It was something I was passionate about, and really intrigued by the concept of becoming psychologically aware. It became like a drug to me. I became almost as addicted to that as I was to music. Not only going into therapy, but reading books on psychology, reading books on the human condition, reading books on . . . just voraciously reading. By default, it was helping me in my situation.' She also talks of her need for 'intellectual intercourse' and even compares herself to Estella, the femme fatale from Charles Dickens' novel *Great Expectations*.

As with many of the other songs on the album, the repetitive riffing of Glen's guitar and the straight drum beats provide a necessarily plain platform for Alanis' more complicated vocal lead. On this track her undulating, oddly wavering voice is in full flow, reaching a dramatic wail

'Most of the songs are, in a roundabout way, actually addressed to myself: there's a certain aspect . . . that's very confessional, very unadulterated.'

at the end of each chorus. It is a very direct and passionate opener, even though it came very late on in the sessions: '"All I Really Want" was written right near the end of the record, and I had been in Los Angeles for a while when I had seen certain things that I didn't necessarily like and some that I did, and that's what the song was based on.'

Next on the album comes the aural and emotional assault of the single 'You Oughta Know'. Coming as it does so early in the record, it is a jarring introduction to just how deep Alanis is prepared to go in her personal exposure, and also emphasises the paradox between the album's sensitive issues and frequently hard rocking backdrop. In direct contrast comes 'Perfect', perhaps the album's most sad yet beautiful song. Some saw this as a resentful but understated tirade against excessive parental authority, even going as far to suggest that Alanis' folks were indeed the archetypal showbiz horror parents, vicariously living their own failed dreams through their offspring. It is easy to see why this interpretation was popular, with the lyrics chiding the child Alanis, expecting nothing but perfection from the youngster, and constantly telling her she is not good enough. Love is offered only in exchange for flawless behaviour and achievement.

Alanis had always spoken very warmly of her parents, however, publicly praising their 'unconditional support' and openmindedness. In answer to these claims of oppressive parental expectations, she said the song was actually about the unspoken pressures of her childhood career, many of which were brought upon her by herself or society. She admitted that no family is 'dysfunction free' but was keen to point out it was an important song for her: 'Finally I had this opportunity to be honest, in many ways for what seemed like the first time. A lot of it came out because I had been repressing it for so long.' In singing this, Alanis' voice trembles with emotion, the simple musical backing, with the occasional Hammond organ and soft guitar, building up momentum as the song draws to its more rocky climax, whereupon the parental disapproval goads the child once more.

An easy-going track follows, the future chart topping 'Hand In My Pocket', where Alanis reflects on the disillusionment and discontent she felt when she first moved to Los Angeles and found herself mugged, penniless and without artistic motivation. Again the music is essentially very simple, with a keyboard bass line and drum machine creating a skipping, infectious rhythm. 'There is always a part of me that is still very introverted,' she says in *Rolling Stone*, 'when I first moved to L.A., I went through a very difficult adjustment period, and I was extremely stressed out, close to having a nervous breakdown.'

After the bouncy melancholy of 'Hand In My Pocket' comes 'Right Through You' in which Alanis angrily abuses the record company executives that she had to endure whilst touting for a record deal. She talks of these men mispronouncing her name (as often happened) and yet claiming to know all about her and lambasts the superficial way the business pigeon-holed her as too young, and wanted to package her cleavage more than her music. She even looks forward to the day when she will have 'zillions' of dollars from her success, a dream she often had when she wrote this song sleeping on friend's couches in L.A. whilst penniless. The song ends abruptly with her laughing at the vanity of these executives who behave so odiously and then scour artists' album credits looking desperately for their name. It is a much harder track than its predecessor, ploughing from the mild acoustic introduction into a tougher, more savage landscape which perfectly fits this scathing account of the infamous casting couch. Alanis later revealed she had exactly seven executives in mind when she wrote the song, and also admitted to having a dream that one of them had left a message on her answerphone in tears after hearing the song.

Nestled in the middle of the album is 'Forgiven', a bitter reposte against Alanis' Catholic upbringing. She renounces the predetermined religious beliefs foisted upon her and the utterly outmoded concepts of sin and guilt that cause such emotional difficulty for so many young Catholics. She also scorns the idea that confession and attending Sunday Church make for good Christians. Skipping from quiet verses to loud, crashing choruses, the song reiterates Alanis' complete rejection of established religion, which has been replaced by her own view of spirituality. Despite the potentially cliched subject-matter, there is a genuine anger in her voice, and although the unsettling middle eight and the rather soft metal backing weaken the track's appeal, it is still an interesting introduction to yet another of Alanis' personal demons.

Next up is another classic pop single, the addictive 'You Learn'. Perhaps the most up-beat track so far, the lyrics look at the learning experience that is life, something that the 21-year-old Alanis certainly knew more than most of her peers about: 'A lot of the premises that I write about on this record have to do with certain parts of my past, and a lot of times when I'm immersed in something really difficult I don't realise that there's a lesson in there somewhere, and that it's only in retrospect that I'll realise why I went though it.' The song also contains the album title, referring to the bitter-sweet experiences that have to be swallowed in order to learn and progress.

The next track, 'Head Over Feet' is unique on *Jagged Little Pill* – a positive, upbeat love song. Again, a rather middle-of-the-road rock backing landscapes a confession of deep love, and the realisation by Alanis that it is okay to expect to be treated well by her partner, something that the remainder of the album suggest she is not used to. Despite its subject-matter, the song is far from being a soppy love ballad, with Alanis making a much more direct, blunt admission of her feelings. The track also features her best harmonica solo on the album.

The tempo and tone are brought right down for 'Mary Jane', a stronger song musically than 'Perfect', but no less beautiful. Apart for the simple drum backing, the vocals are left mostly bare, with the occasional musical accompaniment to embellish her powerful and sad voice. Unusually, Alanis sings fairly straight, avoiding the peculiar

On my early records, my vocal style was . . . made to sound flawless over the course of 15 or 20 takes. Whereas on *Jagged Little Pill* . . . It was more of a priority to convey the emotions.

inflections that make her vocal style so distinctive. The lonely protagonist Mary Jane is implied to be an anorexic, but otherwise the song is perhaps the album's most vague track thematically. On the subject of her unusual singing, Alanis informed *Guitar World*, 'My vocal style comes from two things: one, I think, is having sung for a really long time. And the other is letting go of all the stringent rules of singing that I gave into when I was younger. On my early records, my vocal style was sort of the same but a lot more 'perfect', made to sound flawless over the course of 15 or 20 takes. Whereas on *Jagged Little Pill*, among the things that I was rejoicing about was the fact that we weren't being too precious about anything, including the vocals. There weren't a lot of takes. It was more of a priority to convey the emotions.'

'Ironic', which like 'Mary Jane' was to become an international smash hit and award winning single, has a much clearer theme. Oddly enough, however, most of the 'ironic' features of life that Alanis lists in the mid-tempo song are not actually ironic in the literal sense of the word, but this matters little, as the song captivates regardless. With a much fuller musical treatment than its immediate predecessor, the track sees Alanis returning to her trademark wavering vocal style, this time with greater poignancy.

As the album heads towards its end, 'Not The Doctor' talks of Alanis' emotional independence and her rejection of the previous boyfriends she had who seemed to want her merely as an emotional crutch rather than a partner in life. At times she needed such assistance herself, but frequently found herself having to be the stronger one – she describes these men's self-esteem as being like a bottle which is always empty despite her attempts to fill it up. 'Most of the songs are, in a roundabout way, actually addressed to myself,' she told her official Maverick internet homepage, 'there's a certain aspect of the songs that's very confessional, very unadulterated.' The linear and rather repetitive music is softened by a beautiful catchy acoustic hook, with a sweetly mid-paced yet funky rhythm section.

The penultimate track listed on the album is 'Wake Up', one of the most complex musical numbers, with string sections, full drums, heavy guitar riffing and extensive over-dubbed vocals. Thematically vague like 'Mary Jane', the song nevertheless rounds off the record competently, but after the second version of 'You Oughta Know', the final, hidden track, 'Your House' makes it pale in comparison. Unlike most hidden tracks, this secret song is arguably the finest piece on the record. The track tells the tale of a spurned lover who has broken in to her ex-lover's house while he is out and rifles through his belongings, trying on his aftershave, wearing his clothes, playing his Joni Mitchell album, sleeping in his bed and generally soaking up his aura. Her melancholy and sadness are compounded by the discovery of a love letter from his new woman. Vocally, 'Your House' is far superior to anything else on the album, Alanis' powerful and emotion soaked a cappella rendition finally achieving the complete and exemplary performance that previous songs had only hinted at. With 'Your House', Alanis placed herself on a haunting pedestal, if only fleetingly, that few contemporary artists could compete with. Her description of the track to Elvis Duran of WHTZ was somewhat understated: 'It's the emotion of it just lent itself to being sort of isolated. And it's a cappella, so it just has this mood to it, and I thought it would sort of stick out like a sore thumb if it was in the middle of the record.'

Alanis felt this was the only slightly fabricated song on the album, and this may explain its secret location: 'That is the only song on the record that's not 100 percent true,' she confided to *Spin*. 'I was staying in this guy's house in Hollywood and he wasn't there for a week. I remember being overly curious and sleeping in his bed. It felt eerie and unnerving; I also had kind of a crush on him. I get burned at the end of the song because if I had really snooped around as much as I wanted to, it would have been wrong. I probably would have found something I didn't want to find.'

With that the album comes to a close, leaving the listener feeling battered and emotionally drained, yet uplifted and inspired. In *Jagged Little Pill*, Alanis Morissette opens up her emotions for public dissection, laying her very heart and soul open to ridicule. It is a ridicule that never arrives, however, because the manner in which she expresses herself, both lyrically and vocally, is simply stunning. On reflection, both Glen and Alanis remained proud of their work: 'I think all those upheavals, the pain and the trauma of it, we captured it, you know?' Glen told *Rolling Stone*, 'And the joy of it. I wouldn't recommend it to anybody to needlessly challenge themselves, but in this case, all the challenges were necessary to come out the person she is.' Alanis herself was mutually approving: 'He's a true artist. I knew he hadn't had many opportunities to do his own art, to start with a clean slate and do whatever he wanted. He's the kind of person that if there's an artist that needs a song, he can write it. He can write anything. He's perhaps the most talented person I've ever met in music. I think because of our musical pasts they thought we would come out with something quite different than what we did.'

Although the musical side of the record was a little plain and repetitive at times, this could not detract from Alanis' achievement. With *Jagged Little Pill*, Alanis Morissette had produced one of the albums of the year. Now all that remained to be seen was whether the public would agree.

the sexual chocolate

"... everybody has their own way of releasing. My way is through words. Other people get it out of their system by crowd-surfing or slamdancing."

'I was hoping we would sell 250–300,000, and she would get her feet wet. People would at least know what her name was,' Scott Welch later said of Alanis' June 13 1994 album release. Part of the reason for his moderate goals was her anonymity in the States, where this record was being classed, both by the public and the music industry, as her debut album. Alanis was just delighted to have made the record she had, whilst Maverick had only slightly higher expectations than Welch. Strange then, that nine weeks later, *Jagged Little Pill* had become the hottest album in the States and was selling at the rate of 100,000 copies a week, slamming its way up the Billboard Top 100 to the Number 1 slot and staying in the Top 20 for an unbelievable 89 weeks. By the end of the project's incredible shelf-life, Alanis Morissette was the most successful female debut artist of all time.

On its release *Jagged Little Pill* received warm, although not rapturous critical applause, and the general consensus was that it was an accomplished record by a new artist with great potential. However, when the radio stations got hold of it a strange thing started to happen.

The first major station to champion the album was Los Angeles' highly influential alternative station KROQ. Each time they featured a track the phones lit up, just as they had when 'You Oughta Know' was released, and Maverick Records was besieged with enquiries. Once again, fan letters flooded in saying how Alanis had perfectly summed up their angst. Alanis was delighted: 'It's almost like I felt that by my being that introspective, that other people would be compelled to be introspective about their own lives too, and apparently that's what's happening. And that's beautiful for me . . . even outside of music there's nothing more exciting for me than seeing someone growing, or figuring things out, or communicating. And the fact that this record is prompting people to do that is just so satisfying for me.' Even her parents were proud of her naked personal exposure, despite the language and sexual focus: 'They're happy because they know a lot of what I've gone through, and they're happy I got it all out of my system. My Dad called me up when he heard the record and said, "So you're expressing a lot of emotion. That's good." And I laughed and said, "Yeah, I am, to say the least."'

After only seven weeks, the album was at Number 7 in the Billboard charts, and the sales were accelerating with the ever-growing radio play. A week later it went platinum, with 500,000 sales.

A key feature of the success of the album was Alanis' almost constant touring. Sadly, Glen Ballard opted not to tour with her, since his family commitments and other music projects were too demanding of his time. Fortunately, Alanis managed to recruit a band around her that was perfect for the songs she had to play, made up of Nick Lashley, Jesse Tobias, Chris Chaney and Taylor Hawkins.

Lashley was the oldest member of the group, some ten years senior to Alanis, and English-born. His musical background was inevitably soaked in the Beatles, British punk rock bands like the Clash, the Buzzcocks and the Sex Pistols, as well as the more protracted musings of Pink Floyd. A seasoned veteran of various bands, Lashley played guitar in a rock band called King Swamp in the 1980s before moving on to more illustrious gigs such as Chrissie Hynde of the Pretenders. He was also the only married member of the band, with one son, which made the lengthy touring that Alanis undertook somewhat more testing for him than his colleagues. Even so, he found the atmosphere on the road with Alanis very exciting: 'She's refreshingly nice to work with. She encourages us to put our own personalities and our own creativity into the music, which isn't the case when you go on the road as a hired-gun kind of guitarist.'

The other guitarist, Jesse Tobias, came from a slightly more alternative background, having enjoyed a brief but uneventful spell with the Californian funk rock monsters the Red Hot Chili Peppers. He was born in Austin, Texas, and grew up with the sounds of Santana and War on his father's record player, before being galvanised into forming his own bands by the explosion of punk in the late-seventies. His first band was a high school outfit called Mother Tongue who were sufficiently good to move to L.A. to play full time in 1991, the same year that Alanis was

Alanis at the Birmingham NEC, 14 December 1995.

scratching round the city for success. 'We talk about that sometimes,' he told *Guitar World.* 'She dealt with a lot of the same people I did, in both good and bad ways. And we talk about all the weasels and the scenesters, and how we survived all that with our dignity intact.'

Tobias' stint with the Chili Peppers was short-lived: although he was as physically fit and muscle-bound as his new funky colleagues, he never really fitted in with their peculiar and idiosyncratic world and left after two months. In a switch that took him from rock music's most testosterone overloaded band to the spearhead of a new wave of feminist music, he joined Alanis' world tour and left Dave Navarro (who featured on the *Jagged* track 'You Oughta Know') to take his place rather more permanently in the Chili Peppers. Tobias has since immersed himself in hard nineties rock such as Jane's Addiction and Perry Farrell's other project, Porno For Pyros. Within weeks of joining Alanis' entourage he had converted her into a Rage Against The Machine fanatic.

Drummer Taylor Hawkins was a Kurt Cobain lookalike who was the most jokey of the four backing members. Only two years older than Alanis, Hawkins was originally from Laguna Beach and had a relatively small portfolio of previous bands, including a spell in Sass Jordan's backing band with Lashley.

The final member was the bass guitarist Chris Chaney, another Californian, who had previously backed Chris Cross. Hawkins and Tobias were the first to join in audition and clicked immediately, but it took a while before Alanis found the other two: 'I sang three songs with three different people every half-hour for two days straight,' Alanis recalls. 'Those guys stood out. I was auditioning not only their musicianship, but also if they understood what I was singing in my songs. I mean, I never came out and posed the question, "Do you understand where I'm coming from?" But I did get a sense from them as to whether they did. It's a very precious thing to me, the creation of art, and the process I go through to create is something I hold really dear. So I wanted to get a sense that they were excited by it, too.' She may also have had slightly less gracious motives – all four men were physically very fit and extremely good looking. In fact Alanis said that if she wasn't working with them she would have dated all of them, except Nick because he was married!

At first the rehearsals were fairly relaxed, but as the release of the album approached and the news filtered through from the grassroots that the record was about to go nuclear, the band hurriedly practised for the forthcoming world jaunt. As a result, for the first few weeks of gigs they put in rather poor quality performances, but to their credit this was out of haste and not inability, and over the coming months the *Jagged Little Pill* tour transformed itself into an impressive beast. Growing up in public can be painful, but the band, christened 'The Sexual Chocolate' by Alanis, coped extremely well. She was delighted by her choices: 'I didn't want to work with people that had done it for decades, and were just really tired of the touring process. I needed to feel that they had passion. Because I didn't want to deny myself the pleasure of my own greenness, and the

Alanis at Metropolis in Montreal, 30 November 1995.

wide-eyed "in-aweness" that I had. I didn't want to have to suppress that excitement because I was surrounded by people who were sick of the whole thing. But they've all turned out to be just amazing in this band.'

Life on the road was a new experience for Alanis. During her MCA years she had been offered the chance to promote her albums

Your turn: Alanis invites the crowd to sing at the Phoenix Festival, July 1996.

worldwide but had declined, largely because of her age and school work. Now, however, she was desperate to get out there and gig. Alanis had expressed concern about verbalising the emotional outpourings of *Jagged* in front of so many strangers, but once she was up there she found the experience exhilarating: 'All I have to do if I'm out of the trance for even a millisecond is just think of what I'm saying, think of the words flying out of my mouth, and I'm back there,' she explained to *Mojo,* '. . . everybody has their own way of releasing. My way is through words. Other people get it out of their system by crowd-surfing or slamdancing.' Indeed, she felt that this cathartic element was a distinct necessity for her: 'If I wasn't playing every night I'd be dead. I'd explode,' she informed *Q* magazine. 'I'm not doing this to sell records, I'm doing it because I'm 22 and I can. There may be a point where I have a family, I have children and I won't want to be away from them, but what am I away from now? I'm doing it because it's a magical, testing, challenging experience.' She also felt this release was at times a two-way occurance: 'Sometimes on-stage I'm like a mirror, my music becomes less about me and more about what the audience see in me that reminds them of themselves. I sense that some are there to release their own tension and frustration, and that's gratifying.'

The demographics of her audience were unusual – by the time she was topping the charts across the world with her album, there were an extensive cross-section of society attending her gigs – teenagers with their parents, parents on their own, rockers, punks and most noticeably a general majority of women of all ages – at one gig a thirteen-year-old girl complained to a journalist that the cotton candy cost over $2.

If I wasn't playing every night I'd be dead.

Unfortunately, the live show was one area where Alanis' talent seemed a little threadbare. Coming to each show with so few songs meant that *Jagged Little Pill* had every last drop drained out of it (at first there were no new songs, but that was to gradually change). Her appearance on stage was the antithesis of the polished image she projected in her MCA days. She invariably wore a flouncy shirt with her long sleeves undone at the cuff, fingernails painted light blue, over a pair of shapeless, baggy leather trousers and boots. Her hair hung loose and she wore little make-up, as usual. That was fair enough, but it was her performance that really grated. She would flit around the stage shaking her hand by her side frantically, like a screaming child in the middle of a tantrum and grab her stomach in an odd fashion. Onlookers watched as she performed 'spontaneous' skits with the drumsticks, or jumped on the guitarists. She defended her behaviour on stage by telling *Q* magazine: 'A lot of things I do on-stage I think are my way of showing the small amount of uncomfortableness I feel with being that naked. It's a way of holding it in I suppose. There's still a little coward in there somewhere.'

Once the band had been given the chance to jell, the music from the album was reproduced effectively, faithfully and powerfully, albeit with dashes of heavy metal and excessive solos. Ironically, in the light of Tobias' incompatibility with the Chili Peppers, the backing band soon established themselves as something of a macho carnival as well. Shirts were often removed only a few songs in, revealing rippling biceps and six-pack stomachs. Hair was kept suitably long and guitars were pored over with predictable rockist, masturbatory indulgence. At some gigs Tobias performed in only suspenders and swimming trunks, and when the band returned for their encore, they would frequently have stripped down to their underpants.

Alanis' superb voice was always compelling, but the show itself was a bore. Strangely, in direct contrast to the rest of the set was the encore, when Alanis would walk on stage alone and perform a spine-tinglingly brilliant version of 'Your House', the hidden last track from the album. It was a shame the set was not stripped down to her genius of a voice more often.

Once Alanis' fame started to gather pace she demanded on her rider for each venue that the dressing room be 'a peaceful, relaxing atmosphere, with no hard liquor'. Consequently, venue owners rushed around madly filling their grotty backrooms with incense, wall hangings, foliage of all descriptions and perfumed candles. She requested raw vegetables, organic fruit, Baileys Irish Cream, various ginsengs and bottles of spring water by the dozen. Inside this inner sanctum of tranquillity, Alanis would perform yoga or meditate before each concert, usually in the lotus position, whilst the four men would work out so their muscles were suitably ripped. Alanis would read voraciously from texts such as the pseudo-Buddhist *Even Cowgirls Get The Blues,* by Tom Robbins, and avoided tabloid magazines or papers and television. Sometimes, all five of them would gather in a circle, minutes before going on stage, à la *In Bed With Madonna*, and psyche each other up for the gig ahead, their sense of camaraderie galvanised by their 'spiritual' togetherness, and the fact that Alanis had painted all of their fingernails the same colour! ('It's a good excuse to get a guy to put his hand on your knee'.) None of them performed under the

'A lot of things I do on-stage . . . are my way of showing the small amount of uncomfortableness I feel with being that naked.'

influence of drugs, and the tour bus was similarly clean.

The five band members seemed to get on well together. Inevitably, there were times when tensions were rife, but they appeared to be able to deal with this. Alanis was clearly the boss: 'You try to keep it together. You try to have conversations, meditate, do yoga, eat well, sleep enough and read,' she told *Guitar World*. 'It's really important that you're close with the circle of people that you're in, though I'm still the boss and the leader. There are definite boundaries that come along with that, and I respect them. But at the same time, we all have to stick together and help one another out when it's needed. There's a little bit of difficulty, from my perspective, in that there aren't very many females with this group. There's only three of us. So us females really stick together.'

Nick felt Alanis was keeping everything in perspective on the road, despite the ludicrously accelerating media frenzy and her evolving status as a worldwide celebrity: 'If we'd been playing in Paula Abdul's band or something, she'd be staying at a good hotel and we'd be staying at a Day's Inn. In this band, we all stay at the same hotel.' The tour bus was predictably ransacked, covered in rotting food, dried camomile teabags and empty soft drinks cans, while Alanis scribbled hastily on bits of paper, as her manager took hundreds of phonecalls on his mobile seeking interviews, concerts, recording sessions and appearances. Alanis revelled in the toilet humour of her four colleagues, and they even had a 'shag' competition, based on quantity not quality. It was manic but exciting.

Alanis' growing reputation was reflected in the increasing number of big names on the guest list, such as the Artist Formerly Known As Prince and his new wife, Mayte, Steve Tyler of Aerosmith, David Copperfield, and Emmylou Harris. Prince left before the concert was half over and Copperfield provided a particularly cheesy moment backstage after one show, when Alanis thanked him for coming and he replied 'No, thank you for the magic.'

As with any tour that is on the road for nearly two years, there were a fair share of incident and stories along the way. While touring the globe Alanis appeared on *The David Letterman Show* to great applause, played alongside Bob Dylan, Eric Clapton and the Who at the Hyde Park Prince's Trust gig mentioned earlier and even wrote an article in the *New York Times* about her love for music and the impact of Radiohead's awesome song 'Fake Plastic Trees', which she claimed had rekindled her passion for listening to music (she covered the song on tour). Early on, she was also offered a prestigious slot on the infamous Lollapalooza tour, originally the brainchild of Jane's Addiction's Perry Farrell, as a replacement for a pregnant Sinéad O' Connor. When Alanis turned this down, she was criticised as aloof, but that was unfair – she simply did not have the time and was also wary of growing in popularity too soon without any substantial grassroots following, which might leave her in an unstable position similar to that in her earlier MCA days. She did a huge number of corny radio interviews where the DJ was often fixated on the sexual revelations in 'You Oughta Know', choosing to ask for her bra size rather than question her rather more deeply, as she fully justified and probably craved.

It's really important that you're close with the circle of people that you're in, though I'm still the boss and the leader.

Whilst the euphoria surrounding *Jagged Little Pill* seemed almost universal, Australia was unusually quiet. Although album sales had actually been rather high, the reporter from *Channel 3 News* noted how Alanis arrived at Auckland airport with all the trappings of a megastar, but with hardly any fans waiting outside: 'There were no maddening crowds to greet her at the airport. A tired and washed-out Alanis was hustled to her car. One of her minders seemingly disturbed and emotional flailing away with his handbag. Fighting their way through all of six record company people and promoters, they safely made it to the car and headed off towards a secret location.'

The support band for much of the tour was Loud Lucy, whose enigmatic singer Christian Lane, Alanis was rumoured to be dating during the second half of 1996 (she would not comment). Probably the most exciting moment of their gigs with Alanis was when she and the Sexual Chocolate invaded the stage at the end of Loud Lucy's set to shower the crowd with champagne, and play table tennis at the same time! She was also supported by Radiohead and Imperial Drag later on in the tour.

Alanis did not let the incredible success of the album and the whirlwind tour of the world that eventually dragged her across several continents over two years go unmissed. By the end of the mammoth trawl, she was rightfully proud: 'Right now is pretty pinnacle-ish,' she told *Spin*. 'I went to the beach just the other night and I sat on the same rock I sat on when I first moved to Toronto, which was probably the hardest time in my whole life. I remember sitting on that rock in such major pain. And then I sat on it the other night – same rock – and I just went, "Man."'

awards
and
attacks

"I don't believe in competition. Competition makes my stomach turn. I'm not motivated by winning. I'm not motivated by anything other than my own evolution."

The by-now internationally successful album *Jagged Little Pill* yielded yet more hit singles. After the incredible impact of 'You Oughta Know' any further releases would struggle to compete, but it was a sign of Alanis' fame that each one was still a big hit. 'Hand In My Pocket' was accompanied with a video of Alanis' chauffeur driving a Cadillac through a colourful small town parade, surrounded by street performers, dancers and singers, with the singer watching and observing those around her just as she does in the song. 'You Learn' came with Alanis in another car, this time one which crashes, after which she rides a horse, leaps off a bridge, plays basketball, spars a few rounds in a boxing ring and kisses a complete stranger, denoting a host of weird experiences from which she could learn. But the video and single which had the biggest impact after the album's release was easily 'Ironic'. Four different versions of Alanis ride in the same car, each representing different aspects of her character. She drives and talks to each one of them, from the giggly girl to the darker more contemplative adult, until the end of the video when she stops the car and gets out, whereupon it is revealed to be empty.

✴ ✴ ✴

With so much chart success and touring popularity, it was almost a formality that Alanis' incredible rise to fame would be capped by a glut of music industry awards. Easily the most prestigious of these was the amazing four Grammys she scooped at the celebrated 38th ceremony at the end of February 1996. The evening was dominated by *Jagged Little Pill*. Alanis performed a rousing version of 'You Oughta Know' that had Michael Jackson giving her a standing ovation, before walking off with Best Album, Best Rock Song, Best Rock Album and Best Female Rock Vocal awards. Interestingly, 'You Oughta Know' was the first song in the history of the awards to be nominated with an expletive in it, and similarly became the first such track to win.

After the Grammys came another cupboard full of awards at the 25th annual Juno Awards in Ontario, the Canadian equivalent of the Grammys. Then she dominated the American Music Awards with yet more accolades for Best Album and Best Female Artist – this time she wasn't even in the country, instead leaving Paula Abdul to collect the award on her behalf. This was an impressive haul, especially considering the presence of the Beatles mighty *Anthology* albums and another global seller from mega-popular female singer Mariah Carey.

In the wake of these awards, the album sold even more heavily – in the weeks after the Grammys, *Jagged Little Pill* shifted over 200,000 copies per week, and Maverick Records' freelance promotional rep, Ken Ornberg, took more phone calls about Alanis than for any previous artist he had dealt with, including Eric Clapton. She enjoyed similar success at the MTV Awards, where her Best Video by a New Artist, Best Editing and Best Female Video.

Alanis also dominated the Internet, where 'Ironic' was voted the Best Single of 1996 by music fans on-line (Alanis has chatted on-line with fans three times). She was also chosen as the third Best Entertainer of the year by the big selling *Entertainment Weekly*, and acknowledged as the eighth biggest grossing tour star, with over $23 million in ticket sales.

It was only fair that Glen was also recognised, which he was with the highly prestigious Songwriter Of The Year Award at The American Society of Composers, Authors, and Publishers 14th Annual Pop Music Awards. Another songwriting association, the NARAS, bestowed him with their own highest accolade, the Governor's Award.

The only strange event in the aftermath of these successes was Alanis' failure to mention them at any of the many concerts she was playing around this time (the day before the Grammys she moved out of her L.A. home and placed all her belongings in storage, calling herself a 'nomad'). Several venue owners presented her with Grammy shaped cakes which she politely accepted, but no allusion was made to the awards themselves.

1996 saw Alanis win numerous awards.

This was because she saw little point in such artistic scrummages, as she explained to *Guitar World*: 'I don't believe in competition. Competition makes my stomach turn. I'm not motivated by winning. I'm not motivated by anything other than my own evolution. When I was younger, I always used to think that if you were to have a Number 1 record and win a Grammy award, your life would be wonderful. Your self-esteem would sky-rocket and everyone would love you. But the opposite is true. It's more of a test of you. If your foundation is shaky, then being thrown into that lifestyle will break you.' Tobias confirmed this: 'I remember seeing her throw a Brit and Echo award into her suitcase like they were books she got at the airport. In the end, it's the show that counts. That's probably the biggest trophy of all, when the kids from high school actually tell her their heart is with her.'

Despite her reservations, the awards success around the globe continued to have a remarkable effect on the longevity of *Jagged*. Sales of the album had passed the 14 million mark, 9.5 million of which were in the US alone, and she had rushed past the 12 million mark in only 15 months, by then reaching the Top Ten album listings in over a dozen countries. Incredibly, after seventy weeks on the charts, the record jumped back to Number 1 with sales of another 120,000.

Although the album was actually her third, the industry figures were calling it her debut, as the previous two records were not released internationally. As a result, Alanis was now catapulted into the lofty heights of pop legend alongside some of the all-time greats. She surpassed her heroine Madonna's debut album sales, as well as beating all the Material Girl's other long player successes as well. After the release of the singles, some radio stations were still so anxious for more Alanis music that they started playing 'Head Over Feet' on constant rotation, even though it had not been officially pushed as a single.

If Maverick's projections for her success in South America and the Pacific Rim come true, plus sales continued as expected in the rest of the world, Alanis' success will become even more startling. The biggest-selling debut album ever was Boston's eponymous record, closely followed by Whitney Houston's 1985 debut, which was also the leading female effort. Alanis has already surpassed Houston, and the ultimate top position is within her sights.

*   *   *

The Grammys were notable for a reason other than Alanis' success – the prevalence of female artists, with nominations for Annie Lennox, Björk, Joan Osborne, Dionne Farris, TLC and Bonnie Raitt. In the category of Best New Artist, women outnumbered men by four to one, and the same applied to the Best New Album section. Music has long been a painfully male domain, and since the evolution of popular music, women have struggled to be taken seriously or given the credit they rightly deserve. Alanis was now at the forefront of a new wave of diverse and prodigious female talent, which was no longer fitting the neat sexist pigeon-holes that the patriarchal music business preferred to place them in. TLC were bringing a new rough R&B to the mass market of MTV, Joan Osbourne offered a new country slant and Björk's highly individual music and outrageous personality was another exciting breakthrough after years with the brilliant Sugarcubes. Whilst Whitney Houston and Mariah Carey's eye-lash fluttering and pouting did little for feminism's progress, artists like these were dictating their success on a grand scale. Their discussion of sexuality was a key feature, with Alanis following in the path of Madonna and Salt N' Pepa in being so forthright about her views and experiences (although not as directly candid). Some have suggested that female artists broke through in this year because male music was getting stale, but that is to suggest that if men had been more creative women would not have achieved so much – nonsense, of course. Artists like Alanis won so much acclaim because of the sheer quality of their music, independent of men's failures, or the industry's prejudices.

Alanis gladly acknowledged female influences on her success, especially the genius Tori Amos, whose chilling *Little Earthquakes* is one of the most emotionally vulnerable and unsettling albums ever recorded. Amos' confessional style was far more harrowing than Alanis' material, recounting as it did the horror of being raped as a teenager, but even then it was criticised for being too intense – even so, Alanis found her work inspirational: 'I would defend Tori's honour to the grave. [Critics of her] are not on her wavelength . . . and I'd doubt that she'd want to have a glass of wine over dinner with them.'

Even in the light of such progress, men continued to cast inaccurate aspersions on these artists, including Alanis. She was highlighted as the figurehead of the 'angry women in rock' fashion, and the track 'You Oughta Know' used as the only evidence that she was a sexually aggressive, overtly feminist character – the lines about fucking and going down on her man in a cinema were especially held up as proof. With regard to this, Alanis told Fred Shuster: 'The song was more vulnerable than upset or angry. Anger is an extension of hurt, to me. It's a cowardly way of dealing with pain. When I sing the song now, I think back to the original emotion. The acoustic version with strings at the Grammys was my way of carrying it back to its first emotion, feeling hurt and confused. So, when I see the Angry Young Woman label, it's completely missing the point of what the song is about.'

'Anger is an extension of hurt, to me. It's a cowardly way of dealing with pain.'

Although *Jagged* was indeed sexually very direct, to take this one track as being wholly indicative of Alanis' complete persona is simply wrong: 'The record is my story,' Morissette told Harris Allan of radio station 102.7 WNEW. 'I think of the album as running over the different facets of my personality, one of them being my sexual self. To isolate 'You Oughta Know' is a misrepresentation of the whole story. By no means is this record just a sexual, angry record. That song wasn't written for the sake of revenge, it was written for the sake of release. I'm actually a pretty rational, calm person.' She also felt the media were making too much of her venomous lyrics, again in order to label her: 'That's what people are misconstruing,' she told Julene Snyder. 'Because of the anger and how cutting some of the lyrics are, they presume that I Federal Express these songs to the people they're about and force them to listen to it.'

Alanis was keen to shed the 'Poster Girl For Rage' label that one critic gave her. She was being paraded as the feminist artist your mother liked, the acceptable side of female emancipation, completely patronising and inaccurate on all counts. Alanis had made a point of not using her good looks and femininity to promote her career – the album cover shot was rather oblique and several of her videos were either elusively blurred or filmed in stark lights with little or no make-up. 'My whole philosophy on life is that I'm not about my external appearance,' she extolled. 'What I have to say is far more important than how long my eyelashes are. It's always been that way. I would hate myself if I wound up doing things that were very glamourous – unless I was kidding. I know what it feels like to have that be the priority, 'cause I was once in a position where it was all about my cleavage and look.'

Some observers compared her to critically acclaimed artists such as Melissa Etheridge, Liz Phair, and Polly Harvey, and fellow female performers were quick to applaud, but Alanis was not so convinced of the impact she was having: 'What's happened to me has propelled me into a position where I have to be more verbal about my feminism. But I have had female artists coming up to me and saying "Yeah we're taking over", and I shake my head and say "No, we're not, we're joining."' One female singer who was not so convinced was the colossal egotist Courtney Love, wife of the late Kurt Cobain. She denounced Alanis as a sell-out and claimed she was merely pandering to a male industry and not actually confronting anyone with her radio friendly rock. Love was particularly narrow-minded about Alanis' collaboration with the otherwise mainstream Glen Ballard – 'Tell Alanis she sucks' she shouted after the Grammy Awards. This attack was of course, a little rich coming from a woman who once said, 'I fake it so real, I am beyond fake'. Alanis dealt with this rather tiresome intervention with creditable aplomb: 'Glen has worked with artists in the past that have asked him to create something for them. And [people] have every reason to believe that this has happened again. But Glen and I are so peaceful with this. I can't control people's brains out there.'

Love's pathetic outburst was not the only voice of dissent during 1996, however. As Alanis' success continued to gather pace, the numbers of critics increased, seemingly in proportion. The principal argument was that same as Love's, that Alanis was fabricated, that her collaboration with Glen was no less fake than a thousand glossy pop hits, and that her persona of angry young woman was calculated to hit the market just when it was most susceptible to such an onslaught. Sales figures in the millions were used as evidence that Alanis was never truly alternative, and her contrived touring set-up shown as further proof that she was merely a marketing man's creation (they seemed to ignore the endless rounds of promos and PA's she had done in her MCA days). Some even suggested it was all the brainchild of Madonna herself. Alanis replied to Harris Allen, 'We were very insulated when we were writing the record. So the last thing that I was thinking about was how it was going to be received, let alone whether it was going to be received this well.' Glen was equally adamant: 'All I know is what really happened. And this was the least calculated thing I've ever done,' he proudly explained to *Entertainment* magazine. 'All of her vocals were done the same day the song was written. Singers always want to nuance, but she was so close to what she was saying, singing the lyrics as she wrote them, that at the end of the night I would toss a track on tape as quickly as I could get it there, and she would sing it in one or two takes – and that's the record, largely. That's never happened in my career. I've spent a month just on one vocal.' He also said in *Rolling Stone,* I didn't know where we were going with it. We had our hands on the Ouija board, man, and I'm telling you it just took off . . . The last thing we were trying to figure out was what we were supposed to do in terms of the marketplace.'

When I did the *Rolling Stone* and *Spin* articles, I hadn't really gotten my bearings yet. I was, perhaps, subtly misrepresenting myself because of how new all this was.

Secondly, people complained that she was shamefully disowning her first two albums, further evidence that the *Jagged* phase was a false dawn. It is true that the records are very difficult to get hold of, with rare imports being snapped up and even numerous shoddy bootlegs being made available. As for the rumours that Maverick Records went around the US buying up all stock of *Alanis* and *Now Is The Time* on instructions from Alanis herself, that seems unlikely. On this point Alanis explained to David Wild, 'There was an element of me not being who I really was at the time, it was because I wasn't prepared to open up that way. The focus for me then was entertaining people as opposed to sharing any revelations I had at the time. I had them, but I wasn't prepared to share. No, I'm not scared people might hear those records. I never did *Playboy* centerfolds. There's nothing I regret.'

Thirdly, there was much criticism of her refusal to do interviews at a time when her worldwide success made her such a hot topic, although how this made her fake is questionable. Apart from a *Rolling Stone* and *Spin* article, she did a negligible amount of press during her entire world tour, fuelling rumours that she was a recluse. She had even declined to give interviews at the heavily attended after-show press conference at the Grammys. When the angry media challenged Glen Ballard with this, saying it was arrogant, he said rather oddly that it was justified because they both worked 'outside of the music industry system'. He also offered up the fact that she was 'exhausted' – strangely, she recovered from her acute weariness to attend an all-night party at the Ambassador Hotel after the show. This behaviour particularly infuriated the dozen Canadian reporters waiting backstage, who had been snubbed by Alanis' insistence on only giving interviews to American journalists. Their knowledge of her pop princess past made them even more sceptical. In her defence Alanis told Paul Cantin, 'When I did the *Rolling Stone* and *Spin* articles, I hadn't really gotten my bearings yet. I was, perhaps, subtly misrepresenting myself because of how new all this was. And they are the only journals of record. Because as soon as I knew who I was, I stopped giving interviews. As soon as I became exactly who I knew myself to be all along, I stopped talking to people. So that's people's only recollection of me, what they saw in *Spin*.' Ironically, her withdrawal from the public eye only fuelled the already feverish media hunger for stories on her. The *Daily News* responded in vicious fashion to her repeated refusal to be interviewed with an article announcing 'She does the Trite thing.'

Fourthly, people attacked her allegedly fake Haight-Astbury looks and her occasionally ludicrous L.A. therapy-speak. Take this quote: 'I know the beautiful spirits I would connect with the most, that are listening to my music just for the sake of listening to my music. It makes them think. They don't come up to me. They are not very verbal. They are the ones that watch the show and go, "wow, cool", and then go home and kiss their dog. Everyone else is very loud. Light energy is not very loud.

Alanis at a press conference in Ottawa, 8 March 1996.
The media became increasingly hostile to her as her fame grew.

I'll take you off on this trip with me for a minute here: light energy is not very loud. Darkness is very, very loud.' She also said in all seriousness to Paul Cantin: 'I do a lot of yoga. Getting centred. It takes me to what I call the fourth dimension, it brings me back to the truth. And the truth is not what has come along with all this craziness. The external world is not the fourth dimension, it's a lot of illusion.' Her conversations were littered with the words 'aura', 'energy', 'magic', and 'spiritual', and journalists perhaps understandably tired of this New Age language.

For her part, Alanis was initially upset by all the backstabbing, but as time passed, she became more used to the snipes. She had been riding a rollercoaster of success barely matched in recent years, so it is a tribute to her maturity that she was able to maintain any degree of focus: 'I said to myself that it's time to get centred again. Because it's pretty overwhelming when all of this happens. It's seductive, it tries to pull you away from your centre. As soon as I felt myself being pulled away from it, I said "I've got to start meditating and thinking and talking deeply and writing in my journal." And it brought me back.'

Her manager Scott Welch was less understanding: 'The thing that people are really unforgiving about, that I just wish people would sit back [and realise] you go through a major change in your values, everything, from the time you are 16 to 21,' he said in *Rolling Stone*. 'You move out of the house, you realise everything your parents said wasn't true. People refuse to give her that space.'

On the Internet, where dozens of homepages are dedicated to Alanis' life and work, there waged a fierce war between those believing the conspiracy theory and the ardent fans. One page was set up called PAAMM, or People Against Alanis Morissette's Music, but had to be withdrawn after receiving hundreds of furious e-mails, culminating in a series of death threats.

Alanis the recluse was not so worried about such nasty attacks against her – she no longer read any newspapers, never watched television, and stopped attending any media events of any description. She has said she doesn't mind waiting for the media to take her seriously, and has used the pop bubblegum of George Michael's Wham! days as evidence. Some of the remarks about Alanis may be truthful, particularly the mocking of her L.A. pretension, but generally for such a young person, she has answered her numerous critics adeptly and with grace, and has admirably managed to avoid being disheartened or drawn into an ugly street fight. With album sales approaching the 25 million mark, it seems she doesn't need critical acclaim.

the death of cinderella

"I know there are a million more songs,
and a million more revelations and thoughts
and confusions that I haven't even begun to
write about yet."

As the world tour for *Jagged* came to a close and the album sales finally started to calm down (although they remained relatively high), Alanis took part in a number of unusual events. In June 1997, she played alongside Blur, Björk, Michael Stipe, Noel Gallagher, Sheryl Crow, Tom Petty, Radiohead, Sonic Youth and a host of other acts, in the Tibetan Freedom Concert in New York City. The concert was intended to raise awareness of the plight of Tibet in the wake of Chinese repression, and Alanis also signed a letter to the Vice President Al Gore protesting about the inhumane treatment of various Tibetan followers of the Dalai Lama. She was also pencilled in for a huge international festival called Celebration 2000 which will take place on the six weeks leading up to New Year's Eve at the end of the millenium. The promoters are hoping to book names like Bruce Springsteen, Barbra Streisand, Whitney Houston, Elton John, Bette Midler, Mariah Carey, U2, Pink Floyd, and Genesis. There are also rumours she is provisionally booked for the next series of MTV's popular *Unplugged* shows, which with a voice like hers, would be simply stunning. Rather more comically, on 8 March 1997, she was given the freedom of Ottawa city by the Mayor Jacquelin Holzman who declared it 'Alanis Morissette Day', to which the singer modestly replied she would have preferred 'Alanis Morissette Moment'. That afternoon she announced plans for a Canadian concert tour that may finally heal the wounds between herself and her home country.

With the tour finally over (a fascinating insight is provided in her own comprehensive camcorder diary of the time on the road, *Jagged Litle Pill, Live*), Alanis' chief wish was to 'enjoy some peace and quiet', but this was undermined when both Jesse Tobias and Taylor Hawkins left her band. Tobias had had enough of the touring lifestyle, whilst Hawkins had joined the Foo Fighters, the band of his old friend, Dave Grohl. Although both men had been writing with Alanis on the road a little, it is unlikely that they will take part in the material for her follow-up album.

In many ways, Alanis Morissette faces an odd future. With such a phenomenal and history making 'debut' album behind her, it could be said that the only goal that she has yet to achieve is to avoid being a one-hit wonder. She has said that she imagines Glen will be heavily involved in the process once again with the album being provisionally titled *Fret Bored*, but has hinted that the themes may be somewhat different: 'I think these 13 songs have only just scratched the surface. An author can write about 20 books and still not feel he's written his first. At the moment I'm still trying to get used to the power that I have, the power that just by default comes along with having a successful record.' She continued in *Rolling Stone*: 'All I can promise is I'm going to write exactly where I'm at. I may lose a few people in my audience. Or I may gain some . . . I can't say . . . I know there are a million more [songs], and a million more revelations and thoughts and confusions that I haven't even begun to write about yet.' She also said in *Guitar World* that she would feature, 'Just people, observations. I haven't always written from that autobiographical, self-indulgent place, you know. I've written from some more creative places, some more imagery-based . . . places. *Jagged Little Pill* just came from where I was at that time. That time of my life happened to be one where I was letting out a lot of things that I had repressed for a long time. So I feel like that was a new beginning point for me, as far as the fearlessness involved in creating something that vulnerable. I've written a lot of stuff in the past, but it was all very safe. Because I was nowhere near being as secure a person as I am now.'

Snippets of the future record could be heard on the latter part of the world tour. 'King Of Intimidation' appears to be a continuation of 'You Oughta Know', dealing with the myriad difficulties men and women have in relating to each other. 'Death Of Cinderella' is a heavy guitar track which is largely autobiographical, whilst 'No Pressure Over Capuccino' is written about her brother Wade. There is also an as yet untitled song about the rather un-rock 'n' roll subject of weekends. Then there is

'Can't Not' which highlights the pressures and unreal environment that worldwide fame has brought to Alanis.

Some of the writing for the new album was done on the road but Alanis found the claustrophobic surroundings curtailed her creative ability, as she explained: 'I can't write the kind of lyrics I write with 50 people walking around, setting up the venue. It's too vulnerable for me to

'I'm still trying to get used to the power that I have, the power that . . . comes along with having a successful record.'

do that. I have a hard time writing lyrics in soundcheck. I write melodies in a heartbeat. But in order to go to that place spiritually – that stream-of-consciousness, unfettered, unjudged place where I write lyrics from – I need to be somewhere a little less public.' To help her, they shipped in a mini-band set-up which would be placed in a back room of each venue, where she and the band could jam together, although not always that successfully. Her on-the-road songwriting endeavours were made all the more difficult when a duffel bag containing some tapes of new songs was stolen, although much to her relief it was returned anonymously a few weeks later.

The most successful female debut artist of all time.

She has also expressed a wish to pursue other areas of her life than music. She talked to the *Dayton Daily News* of a desire to return to her childhood thespian activities: 'I'm definitely going to delve back into acting at some point, if for no other reason than just to get into another character because I've had to talk about myself and sing about myself and write about myself for the last year or so. It would be challenging to get back into another character and do something I did when I was younger, and I've gotten so far away from it that it scares me again. I love doing things that scare me. Because it makes me feel alive and challenged. It makes me feel like I'm growing. That comfort-zone area, I hate it. Not all of us can be out of our comfort zone 24 hours a day. For whatever reason, I'm happiest when I'm out of my comfort zone.' There was also a rumour that she wanted to become the J. D. Salinger of the music world. Salinger wrote the classic novel *The Catcher In The Rye*, then retired to a New Hampshire redwood cottage, where he continued to write in seclusion, solely for his own amusement. Alanis hates much of the furore that comes with being a megastar, so this idea may have briefly appealed, but once she is out of the whirlwind of tour dates and promotional schedules, she will no doubt be hankering after yet more music.

In the meantime, Maverick Records have announced the next album will probably not be released until Summer 1998 and, until then, Alanis will not be performing or speaking in public.

+ + +

On Alanis Morissette's 21st birthday she played a concert in front of 300 people. On her next birthday, she performed to 3,000, and with another 2,000 who couldn't get hold of tickets. Her rise to fame was certainly meteoric, although it didn't happen overnight, as people realised when they became aware of her painful experiences in the MCA pop years. For someone who is not yet in her mid-twenties, Alanis displays a remarkably wise head and workaholic dedication, and to have enjoyed the historical success she has and stayed reasonably together is a tremendous achievement. Maybe her next album will flop; more likely it will be another hit. Essentially, she has already made an impressive mark.

For those men who spurned her and provided her with much of the material for *Jagged*, she has a warning: 'I'm never going to get dumped again.' For the legions of females who now aspire to be her, she is even more pragmatic: 'Don't ever mistrust those voices in your head. Because they're always there and I just ignored them. And take off all that make-up. And the heels."

Early recordings

Fate Stay With Me
Independent Label
Canada
Fate Stay With Me

Albums as Alanis

Alanis
MCA Records 1992
Canada
Feel Your Love
Too Hot
Plastic
Walk Away
On My Own
Superman
Jealous
Human Touch
Oh Yeah!
Party Boy

Now Is The Time
MCA Records 1992
Canada
Real World
An Emotion Away
Rain
The Time of Your Life
No Apologies
Can't Deny
When We Meet Again
Give What You Got
(Change Is) Never a Waste
   of Time
Big Bad Love

Albums as Alanis Morissette

Jagged Little Pill
Maverick/Reprise 1995
USA
All I Really Want
You Oughta Know
Perfect
Hand In My Pocket
Right Through You
Forgiven
You Learn
Head Over Feet
Mary Jane
Ironic
Not The Doctor
Wake Up
*You Oughta Know
**Your House (2:58)

* Later releases of the album have
* this extra version of You Oughta Know*
** Unlisted Track

Singles

You Oughta Know
Maverick/Reprise 1995
England
You Oughta Know
(Clean Album Version)
You Oughta Know
(Jimmy the Saint Blend)
Perfect (Acoustic Version)
Wake Up

Hand In My Pocket
Maverick/Reprise 1995
England
Hand In My Pocket
Head Over Feet
(Live Acoustic)
Not The Doctor
(Live Acoustic)

You Learn
Maverick/Reprise 1996
England
You Learn
Your House (live in Tokyo)
Wake Up (Modern Rock Live)
Hand In My Pocket

Ironic
Maverick/Reprise 1996
USA
Ironic (album version)
Forgiven (Live)
Not the Doctor (Live)
Wake Up (Live)*

Notable Bootlegs

Intellectual Intercourse
In Concert and Beyond 1995
Germany

Rockin' the Ford
Tornado 1995
USA

The Girl With the Thorn in Her Side
Forbidden Fruit 1995
England

Miss Thing
1995
Holland

Going North
Moonraker1995

Tune In, Turn On, Drop Out
Moonraker 1996